Advance Praise for *Rediscovering the American Covenant: The Duty Is Ours*

"Mark Burrell's book *The Duty Is Ours* is tremendous! It is thoroughly researched and excellently written, packed with valuable information to educate Americans on our amazing heritage of individual freedom and liberty. This insightful volume highlights the powerful biblical wisdom and truths the founders drew from to create our unique 'government from the consent of the governed.' You will appreciate more your Creator-given rights and responsibilities after reading Mark's work. I recommend this powerful resource."

—William J. Federer, nationally known speaker, bestselling author, *American Minute* radio host, and president of Amerisearch, Inc. Publishing

"I highly recommend the writings of Mark Burrell. He has the great ability to present ideas of government, history, and theology in a cogent and accessible way that is so valuable for modern Christians. A theology of civil government is mostly lacking in the American church today, but this book will help to bring it back. There are few books that I can wholeheartedly endorse, and this is one of the few. Every pastor needs it, and I pray that it becomes a Bible study tool in many churches."

—Mark Beliles, president of American Transformation Company; pastor emeritus at Grace Covenant Church in Charlottesville, Virginia; and founder of Providence Foundation

"Many Americans—and I'm one of them—feel we're heading in the wrong direction as a nation. It's time to get back to our founding principles. What were they? They can be seen in the Mayflower Compact and the Declaration of Independence, among other documents. Mark Burrell's book reminds us of our need to recommit to the legacy of liberty bequeathed to us Americans by the settlers and founders of America."

—Dr. Jerry Newcombe, author of *The Book That Made America* and co-author (with Peter Lillback) of *George Washington's Sacred Fire*

THE DUTY
IS OURS

REDISCOVERING THE
AMERICAN COVENANT

THE DUTY
IS OURS

MARK BURRELL

Ballast Books, LLC
www.ballastbooks.com

Copyright © 2024 by Mark Burrell

Unless otherwise noted, scripture quotations are from The Holy Bible, New International Version®, NIV® Copyright © Biblegateway.com. Used by permission. All rights reserved.

Abbreviations According to The SBL Handbook of Style, 2d ed., 2014.

Words that are italicized in quotes are used for the author's emphasis and are not italicized in the quotation's source.

ISBN: 978-1-962202-49-7

Printed in the United States of America

Published by Ballast Books
www.ballastbooks.com

For more information, bulk orders, appearances, or speaking requests, please email: info@ballastbooks.com

ACKNOWLEDGMENTS

To my family and friends who helped with editing this book: Laurie Pappas, Connie Stradling Morby, and Charlene Burrell.

To those continuing to encourage me with this unique ministry aimed at helping the church rediscover the citizenship role all Christians have in the nations and communities where they live.

To my dear wife Charlene, for her continued support in completing these book projects.

And lastly,

To all American patriots currently living out their pledge to preserve our precious American covenant, the Declaration of Independence, by *committing their lives, fortunes, and sacred honor.*

TABLE OF CONTENTS

INTRODUCTION

August 13, 1983, was one of the most important days in my life. On that day, I married Charlene St. Clair in Factoryville, Pennsylvania. We have gone on to have four kids and six grandchildren, and we hope for more! When I look back on that day over forty years ago, the magnitude and significance of the event are much more apparent in my mind. We followed the process that nearly every couple of faith follows on their wedding day, which consists of four basic steps: we acknowledged God and His purpose for holy matrimony, we appealed to God to bless the marriage, we committed to it by exchanging vows and rings, and we declared to the world that from that day forward, we are Mr. and Mrs. Mark and Charlene Burrell. In performing these tasks, we were making a marriage covenant following God's template for covenant making.

Covenants are extremely important in the Bible. God takes them very seriously and promises to bless those entering into a covenant if they follow the biblical template. This holds true for marriages as well as for communities and nations. The process Charlene and I followed that day is precisely the process the Pilgrims followed when they realized they could not join the Jamestown colony and decided to start their own settlement.

1

They did what their pastor in Holland had taught them to do: establish a covenant. Before they left the Mayflower, they drafted a simple document that followed the same template, known as the Mayflower Compact.

The American founders also followed this biblical template to initiate the American founding in July of 1776. The document they drafted was not a news bulletin or a "Dear John letter" to King George back in England; it was a solemn agreement following the biblical template based on the commonly shared Christian beliefs of the colonies during that era. Just as God promises to bless a man and a woman making a marriage covenant who follow the biblical template, He promises to bless nations that follow the nation-starting template given to us through the nation of Israel.

We often overlook the remarkable blessings that biblical principles offer because of our busy daily routines. However, if we examine world history and inquire about the most challenging aspect of human existence since recorded times, the answer is evident. The hardest thing for mankind has been to live in peace with one's neighbor, whether it is one's neighbor next door or a neighboring nation. While the modern church tends to be silent about God's plan for nations and the business of governing, the Bible equips us with all we need to know about living harmoniously with all our neighbors, respecting that each person is on their own faith journey. This journey might involve embracing or rejecting the God of the Bible.

America has gone through numerous cycles of distress, often because of not staying true to the biblical principles captured in our founding covenant—the Declaration of Independence. This was especially true in the early 1800s, as the colonies continued to struggle with the institution of slavery. A clear boundary had formed between the North and South during the founding era—the North wanted to abolish slavery, while the South wanted to protect it. One man saw the injustice of slavery and the inconsistency with the principle of equality captured in our Declaration of Independence. That man was John Quincy Adams, the son of the second president, John Adams.

John Quincy Adams served as president from 1825 to 1829, and afterward he was elected to Congress, representing his home state of Massachusetts. He was the only president to hold a significant public office after being president. During his seventeen years as a congressman, he constantly pushed for the abolition of slavery, but most of his fellow members of Congress repeatedly shut him down. His peers even issued a gag order to prevent him from discussing slavery on the House floor. However, this did not stop him, and he became known as the "hellhound of slavery."

He was once asked why he kept bringing up the slavery issue despite years of rejection. He responded, "The duty is ours; results are God's."[1] This sentiment perfectly aligns with what the Bible teaches when Christians encounter injustice around them. They are meant to confront it, ideally restoring those treated unjustly. The Bible is clear that this is what God expects from us (Isa. 1:17; Matt. 23:23), and He will acknowledge those who faithfully fulfill this responsibility, as the writer of Hebrews points out:

> And what more shall I say? I do not have time to tell about Gideon, Barak, Samson and Jephthah, about David and Samuel and the prophets, who through faith conquered kingdoms, administered justice, and gained what was promised; who shut the mouths of lions, quenched the fury of the flames, and escaped the edge of the sword; whose weakness was turned to strength; and who became powerful in battle and routed foreign armies. (Heb. 11:32–34)

As we progress through the twenty-first century, there are political forces attempting to fundamentally transform America away from its founding principles. Instead of celebrating liberty and freedom, the Progressive narrative claims that America is systemically racist and irredeemable. Key institutions are being challenged, and the biblical constructs around marriage and gender are being redefined. Many patriots are questioning what has happened and how we can return to our founding principles.

The founding generation took bold action to confront unjust British rule, viewing it as part of their Christian duty. However, the modern church has largely rejected this doctrine. Most pastors today assert that involvement in politics interferes with evangelism and rarely address it from the pulpit. But does this align with what the Bible teaches? Was John Q. Adams mistaken about our citizenship duty?

In my first book, *Rediscovering the American Covenant: Roadmap to Restore America*, I provided an extensive biblical explanation, arguing that all Christians have a citizenship duty in the communities and nations in which they live. I explained the history leading up to the founding and how America has slowly turned away from this duty during the latter part of the twentieth century. This first book was meant to equip pastors with the strongest biblical argument for active Christian citizenship. I included relevant history and answers to the common objections to "discussing politics" made by today's church. But, while thorough, one friend summarized, "It is dense." That comment prompted me to write the book you are now reading.

In this book, I take a different approach by answering five basic questions all Christians should be asking about their role regarding civil government:

1. What does God expect from the nations of the world?
2. Whom does God call to govern justly?
3. What is the proper response from Christians when being governed justly?

4. What is the proper response from Christians when being governed unjustly?

5. What is the process of restoring a wayward nation back to God?

In this book, I will summarize God's desires and expectations concerning nations, the principles and processes for establishing a nation, governing it justly, and restoring a nation that has gone astray. By addressing these questions, we will come to understand that John Q. Adams was correct regarding the business of civil government and the provision of equal justice for all: "the duty is ours," and "the results are God's."[2]

Throughout history and across the globe, it will always be people of faith whom God expects to step forward to establish liberty and justice for all. There is a timeless biblical blueprint to restore a wayward nation, which means there is hope. Read on to learn the plan God offers, how it has consistently worked in the past, and how we can avail ourselves of it today.

Mark Burrell

CHAPTER 1

GOD'S EXPECTATIONS OF NATIONS

To understand God's plan for civil government, we must look back at God's expectations for the nations that would follow Adam and Eve. After considering His expectations for nations in general, we must address two additional questions: what are the biblical principles and the process for starting a nation, and what does governing a nation justly look like? This first chapter will deal with these three questions.

GOD'S PLAN FOR THE NATIONS

God begins planet Earth by creating Adam and Eve, the first family. Initially, they enjoyed direct fellowship with God in the Garden of Eden, and God tells them in Genesis 1:28 to do the following:

Be fruitful and increase in number; fill the earth and subdue it. Rule over the fish in the sea and the birds in the sky
and over every living creature that moves on the ground.

God had only one condition for the first couple: to not eat
from the Tree of Knowledge of good and evil. Unfortunately, they
broke this rule, leading to God expelling them from the garden.
Since they now knew good from evil, they had a conscience to
help them make day-to-day choices so they could live in a way that
would honor God. After they were cast out of the Garden of Eden,
they went on to have numerous children and populate the world.

After around 1,500 years, the question to ask was: how were
all the people doing? Were they honoring God and living in
peace? Genesis 6 provides the answer:

The LORD saw how great the wickedness of the human
race had become on the earth, and that every inclination
of the thoughts of the human heart was only evil all the
time. (Gen. 6:5)

Now the earth was corrupt in God's sight and was full of
violence. (Gen. 6:11)

As a result, God sent a flood that spared only Noah, his
wife, his three sons, and their wives. As we look toward the
repopulation of the earth taking place through Noah and his
family, several questions come to mind: What would prevent
a repeat of the violent society that existed prior to the flood?
What would give them hope that things could be different?

In Genesis 9 and 10, we see God confirming His original directions for the nations in Genesis 1:28:

> Then God blessed Noah and his sons, saying to them, "*Be fruitful* and *increase in number* and *fill the earth.*" (Gen. 9:1)

God still desired the ensuing nations to *be fruitful, increase in number, and fill the earth.* In Genesis 9:5–6, however, we learn something new; God's desire for justice was intended to keep evil in check going forward and prevent the widespread violence that existed prior to the flood:

> And for your lifeblood I will surely *demand an accounting.* I will *demand an accounting* from every animal. And from each human being, too, I will demand an *accounting* for the life of another human being. "Whoever sheds human blood, *by humans shall their blood be shed;* for in the image of God has God made mankind." (Gen. 9:5–6)

To create an orderly society free from rampant violence as existed prior to the flood, God required humanity to establish a civil authority tasked with punishing those who commit violence against their fellow citizens.

I have never encountered anyone who refutes the idea that this is where God ordained civil government with the objective to maintain law and order. When seeking additional guidance on how to govern in the rest of the Old Testament, we find thousands of verses further describing what a just civil authority should look like. We will elaborate on that later, but all these descriptions converge on the ultimate goal of a civil governing authority: to govern justly. This is how I will summarize the intent behind Genesis 9:5–6 going forward.

Putting all this together, these verses reveal what God desires from the nations that would descend from Noah's family:

- *Be fruitful*
- *Increase in number*
- *Fill the earth*
- *Govern justly*

These verses affirm what God told Adam and Eve in Genesis 1:28, except for the fourth item, which was similar but needed clarification. They were to subdue the earth but were not told how to do it. The purpose of the approximately 1,500-year period before the flood was to prove beyond a shadow of a doubt that mankind needed nations governing justly to live in peace with their neighbors and to have the freedom to choose whether or not to follow God.

Lastly, many years later, God reiterates the same message to Jacob, reminding him that many nations will come from his line:

And God said to him, "I am God Almighty; be fruitful and increase in number. A nation and a community of nations will come from you, and kings will be among your descendants." (Gen. 35:11)

This confirms the consistent message that God anticipated a community of nations to arise. Other Old Testament verses confirm His desire for the nations of the world to follow Him so that they, too, could be blessed:

Therefore, you kings, be wise; be warned, you rulers of the earth. Serve the LORD with fear and celebrate his rule with trembling. Kiss his son, or he will be angry and your way will lead to your destruction, for his wrath can flare up in a moment. Blessed are all who take refuge in him. (Ps. 2:10–12)

Let all the earth fear the LORD; let all the people of the world revere him. (Ps. 33:8)

Blessed is the nation whose God is the LORD, the people he chose for his inheritance. From heaven the LORD looks down and sees all mankind; from his dwelling place he watches all who live on earth—he who forms the hearts of all, who considers everything they do. No king is saved by the size of his army; no warrior escapes by his great strength. A horse is a vain hope for deliverance; despite all its great strength it cannot save. But the eyes of the LORD are on those who fear him, on those whose hope is in his unfailing love, to deliver them from death and keep them alive in famine. (Ps. 33:12–19)

With this in mind, let us unpack what it might look like for a nation to *be fruitful, increase in number, fill the earth,* and *govern justly.*

Be Fruitful

Being fruitful entails being productive and contributing to a nation's growth and prosperity. To achieve this, a just governing authority must promote virtue, which is the pursuit of moral living. A virtuous society requires fewer laws and encourages the development of innovative ideas in all aspects of life. This is because virtuous citizens self-regulate based on their sense of moral duty. Such an environment enables every individual to pursue their interests and reach their full potential, all while bearing in mind their civic responsibility to live in peace with their neighbors.

This responsibility is even more significant for Christians, as they believe God gives His followers abilities and opportunities to serve and bless others so they can be fruitful. This service includes leading in the public arena, ensuring the religious and civil rights of everyone are protected.

Nations thrive when citizens can use their God-given talents in their vocations or recreational pursuits. Educating a society with a biblical worldview leads to recognizing that God created the laws governing the universe. It logically follows that God's laws are knowable and discoverable, which compels those with the necessary intellect to pursue greater knowledge of the world around us. They do this with the belief that learning about science is like learning about God (Jer. 51:15–16; Ps. 111:2). This deeper understanding of science fosters inventions that improve human life and address the challenges of a growing society.

The sixteenth century was a crucial turning point for mankind. Enabled by the invention of the printing press around 1440 and the resulting availability of English Bibles to the masses, people were realizing there was a rational basis supporting the Christian faith. A person could study the Bible through critical thinking to determine its meaning on a topic.

This reasoned approach to the Christian faith spread to scientific fields and led to significant discoveries. Many great scientists of the sixteenth century and onward were Christians, including scientists like Nicolaus Copernicus, Galileo Galilei, Johannes Kepler, Francis Bacon, and Louis Pasteur. Their work drove scientific advances, leading to all the modern conveniences we enjoy today. They spoke openly about how their faith, supported by reason, fueled their passion for decoding the laws of the universe:

> To know the mighty works of God, to comprehend His wisdom and majesty and power; to appreciate, in degree, the wonderful workings of His laws, surely all this must be a pleasing and acceptable mode of worship to the Most High, to whom ignorance cannot be more grateful than knowledge. (Nicolaus Copernicus)[3]

> The laws of nature are written by the hand of God in the language of mathematics. (Galileo Galilei)[4]

> The chief aim of all investigations of the external world should be to discover the rational order and harmony which has been imposed on it by God and which He revealed to us in the language of mathematics. (Johannes Kepler)[5]

For man, by the fall, lost at once his state of innocence, and his empire over creation, both of which can be partially recovered even in this life, the first by religion and faith, the second by the arts and sciences. (Francis Bacon)[6]

The more I study nature, the more I stand amazed at the work of the Creator. Into his tiniest creatures, God has placed extraordinary properties that turn them into agents of destruction of dead matter. (Louis Pasteur)[7]

The primary aim of every government should be to safe-guard the rights of all to enable everyone to pursue their interests and reach their full potential. This creates opportunities for innovators and risk-takers to leverage scientific advancements to enhance the human condition and enjoy the rewards of their endeavors.

Some today say we need more regulations to save the planet, but balancing environmental stewardship with economic policy is essential to leave a better planet for future generations while also allowing a society to thrive. Such governance fosters remarkable progress in the arts and sciences, benefiting the citizens and other nations. It enables nations to flourish and be fruitful.

Increase in Number

God directed the nations to grow in population. Still, one could reasonably question if there is some limit given the approximately eight billion people we have today, with many of them living in poverty. But is this a population problem or a leader-ship problem across nations?

We often witness once-thriving nations, like Venezuela, decline under new regimes while others, like South Korea, liberated from tyranny and following biblical principles, flourish. In America, agricultural innovation has allowed a small percentage of people to feed the vast majority. This shows that feeding the multitudes is possible with the right civil leaders defending liberty and justice for all.

The Bible does not provide a population cap, and America's experience suggests that nations should continue increasing in number as long as they follow God's blueprint for just governance.

Fill the Earth

God's intention was for the nations to spread out across the earth. Genesis 11 tells us how mankind initially wanted to settle together, but God confused their language to prompt them to disperse. It was in the 1400s that the known world comprehended the vast expanse of our planet, leading to the settlement of most of the earth in the subsequent centuries, resulting in approximately 190 separate nations worldwide today. In the twenty-first century, mankind has spread out and filled the earth.

Govern Justly

Having a just civil authority to establish law and order is critical for enabling a productive and flourishing society. It begins with the protection of life, and it is essential to note that God is not merely suggesting its importance—He is demanding it:

> And for your lifeblood I will surely *demand an accounting.* I will *demand an accounting* from every animal. And from each human being, too, I will *demand an accounting* for the life of another human being.

> Whoever sheds human blood, *by humans shall their blood be shed*; for in the image of God has God made mankind. (Gen. 9:5–6)

Notice that God emphasizes this demand three times! Nowhere else in the Bible does God insist on anything from us, not even that we follow Him. Here, however, He unequivocally demonstrates His concern for safeguarding an individual's "right to life."

Given that God created mankind for fellowship and given His demand for an accounting of the shedding of innocent blood, it is clear that He desires to protect every individual's life, providing them the opportunity to consider Him and make their own choice to follow Him.

The Old Testament contains numerous verses highlighting God's profound concern not only for the injustice of murder but also for any form of injustice experienced by citizens. Civil leaders are expected to ensure equal, fair, and impartial justice for everyone in the community, including foreigners from other nations:

Appoint judges and officials for each of your tribes in every town the LORD your God is giving you, and they shall judge the people fairly. Do not pervert justice or show partiality. Do not accept a bribe, for a bribe blinds the eyes of the wise and twists the words of the innocent. Follow justice and justice alone, so that you may live and possess the land the LORD your God is giving you. (Deut. 16:18–20)

Speak up for those who cannot speak for themselves, for the rights of all who are destitute. Speak up and judge fairly; defend the rights of the poor and needy. (Prov. 31:8–9)

How long will you defend the unjust and show partiality to the wicked? Defend the cause of the weak and father-less: maintain the rights of the poor and oppressed. Rescue the weak and needy; deliver them from the hand of the wicked. (Ps. 82:2–4)

Assemble the people—men, women and children, and the foreigners residing in your towns—so they can listen and learn to fear the LORD your God and follow carefully all the words of this law. (Deut. 31:12)

Dozens of verses reinforce God's emphasis on providing civil justice to every individual, regardless of gender, race, class, or nationality. The critical point is that Genesis 9:5–6 teaches us about the citizenship duty that all of mankind has across the nations that would form from Noah's family, which occurs before the nation of Israel is established. This applies whether citizens of these nations are people of faith or not.

It's crucial to understand that without a just civil authority, as was the case before the flood, society becomes increasingly violent, making it challenging to share the gospel. An important lesson to be learned here is that establishing a just civil authority takes priority over evangelism because without law and order, societies always devolve into chaos and, ultimately, tyranny. This means civil government is God's provision to mankind to create an environment not only for people to live in peace and be productive but also to engage in evangelism.

We will explore this further in a later chapter. Still, it is crucial to note that God demands a just civil authority so that people can live in peace, not only to grow in their faith but also to engage with one another, including sharing the gospel. This means that establishing and maintaining a just civil authority is not optional, as many evangelical leaders assert; it is our duty.

The next logical questions are: what is the biblical template for starting a God-honoring nation, and what are the operating principles for governing justly?

THE PROCESS FOR STARTING A NATION

We gain insight into the process of starting a nation in the book of Exodus, specifically in chapters 19–24, when God calls

Moses to lead the Hebrews out of Egyptian bondage. Moses is the author of the first five books of the Bible, often referred to as the Book of Moses, the Book of the Law, or the Pentateuch. These books include Genesis, Exodus, Leviticus, Numbers, and Deuteronomy. This is where we find detailed instructions on establishing a God-honoring nation and ensuring just governance. Through Moses formalizing Israel as a nation, we learn there is a clear blueprint for officially starting a nation. This blueprint consists of four distinct steps:

- *Acknowledge*
- *Appeal*
- *Commit*
- *Declare**

Acknowledge

To initiate a community or nation committed to honoring God, the individuals involved must acknowledge God's supreme authority as the creator of the universe. This recognition should extend to His guiding principles, with His timeless Moral Law as the paramount standard for all legislation. This acknowledgment of God's ultimate authority is prominently outlined in Exodus 19 and 20:

---

* In the case of forming the nation of Israel, the order of these steps is a little different, but I am explaining it in this order here, as it will more directly correlate with the flow of America's founding covenant, the Declaration of Independence.

"'Now *if you obey me fully and keep my covenant,* then out of all nations you will be my treasured possession. Although the whole earth is mine, you will be for me a kingdom of priests and a holy nation.' These are the words you are to speak to the Israelites." So *Moses went back and summoned the elders of the people* and set before them *all the words the* LORD *had commanded him to speak. The people all responded together,* "We will do everything the LORD has said." (Exod. 19:5–8)

And God spoke all these words: "I am the LORD your God, who brought you out of Egypt, out of the land of slavery. *You shall have no other gods before me.*" (Exod. 20:1–3)

When the people saw the thunder and lightning and heard the trumpet and saw the mountain in smoke, *they trembled with fear.* They stayed at a distance and said to Moses, "Speak to us yourself and we will listen. But *do not have God speak to us or we will die.*" Moses said to the people, "Do not be afraid. *God has come to test you, so that the fear of God will be with you to keep you from sinning.*" (Exod. 20:18–20)

In these passages, we witness the Israelites grasping and embracing God's authority and supreme power over them to such an extent that they were gripped by fear for their lives. However, it's important to note that God's intention is not for us to live in fear. Instead, He desires those who seek to establish a nation that honors Him to acknowledge Him as the creator and sustainer of all things and recognize His divine role in the process.

Appeal

The concept of appealing to God is about seeking His assistance. God had previously made an unconditional promise to Abraham many years ago, reaffirming His intention to make Israel a great nation. However, just as with any simple prayer request, God desires His people to ask for His help, as it demonstrates reliance and dependence on Him. In the case of Israel, they sought God's assistance in several ways, first during their period of Egyptian slavery while they waited for God to fulfill His promise to Abraham. This was when Moses had a miraculous encounter with God through the burning bush:

> The LORD said, "I have indeed seen the misery of my people in Egypt. *I have heard them crying out* because of their slave drivers, and I am concerned about their suffering. So I have come down to rescue them from the hand of the Egyptians and to bring them up out of that land into a good and spacious land, a land flowing with milk and honey—the home of the Canaanites, Hittites, Amorites, Perizzites, Hivites and Jebusites. And now *the cry of the Israelites has reached me,* and I have seen the way the Egyptians are oppressing them. So now, go. I am sending you to Pharaoh to bring my people the Israelites out of Egypt." (Exod. 3:7–10)

This passage suggests that appealing to God was the catalyst for His intervention, initiating a series of events that ultimately resulted in the covenant established through Moses.

Second, God instructed Moses to make an altar "and sacrifice on it your burnt offerings and fellowship offerings . . ." (Exod. 20:24). When these sacrifices were made, they were not only being obedient, but they were also appealing to God to forgive their sins as a condition to bless their nation per the covenant they were establishing through Moses.

Commit

The essence of any covenant lies in the willing agreement of all parties involved to adhere to its terms. This involves a clear articulation of the covenant's terms, which took place on Mount Sinai:

> "'Now *if you obey me fully and keep my covenant,* then out of all nations you will be my treasured possession. Although the whole earth is mine, you will be for me a kingdom of priests and a holy nation.' These are the words you are to speak to the Israelites." So *Moses went back and summoned the elders of the people* and set before them *all the words the LORD had commanded him to speak. The people all responded together, "We will do everything the LORD has said."* (Exod. 19:5–8)

Following God's description of many laws He expects the Hebrews to seek to obey (found in Exodus 21–23), the people once more express their commitment to the covenant by willingly consenting to its terms:

> When Moses went and told the people all the LORD's words and laws, they responded with one voice, "Everything the LORD has said we will do." Moses then wrote down everything the LORD had said. (Exod. 24:3–4)

This is the origin of the concept known as the "consent of the governed." The legal validity of any covenant, whether it's a marriage, business agreement, or religious commitment, rests entirely on the principle that the individuals participating in the covenant willingly offer their consent to support and abide by it.

Declare

In the Old Testament era, the final step in ratifying a covenant was to perform a sacrifice and confirm the covenant's terms. This took place in Exodus 24 after God provided more detailed instructions on how He expected the Hebrews to live, as recorded in Exodus 21, 22, and 23:

> He [Moses] got up early the next morning and *built an altar at the foot of the mountain* and set up twelve stone pillars representing the twelve tribes of Israel. Then he sent young Israelite men, and *they offered burnt offerings and sacrificed young bulls as fellowship offerings to the LORD.* Moses took half of the blood and put it in bowls, and the other

half he splashed against the altar. Then *he took the Book of
the Covenant and read it to the people.* They responded, *"We
will do everything the* LORD *has said; we will obey."* (Exod.
24:4–7)

These four steps are the pattern for making any covenant.
Note that these are the same four steps that happen in a marriage ceremony:

1. **Acknowledge** Gods plan for holy matrimony: *". . . We
   are gathered here today in the sight of God and man to join
   these two people in holy matrimony . . ."*
2. **Appeal** to God for His help to strengthen the marriage:
   *". . . to that which God has established, let no man put asun-
   der . . ."*
3. **Commit** to establishing a godly and just home based on
   biblical principles: *". . . I take you to be my lawfully wedded
   wife . . . to have and to hold in good times and bad . . ."*
4. **Declare** your intentions to witnesses attending: *". . . introducing for the first time in public, Mr. and Mrs. . . ."*

Indeed, the process must be identical, as communities
and nations are made up of families. Families, while enjoying
the advantages of residing in a civil society, should collectively
endorse the covenants underpinning their governance. Adhering to these principles guarantees that they are instilling good
citizenship values in their children for the future and invites
God's blessings upon these family units.

Through Israel's example, God has provided a straightforward blueprint for establishing a community or nation that
honors Him. The steps are to *acknowledge* the authority of God's

law, *appeal* to God for assistance, *commit* to the terms of the covenant, and publicly *declare* it. This blueprint guides any group of people aiming to create an institution or nation that honors God. The last question to address is: what does it mean for a nation to govern justly?

PRINCIPLES FOR GOVERNING A NATION JUSTLY

Similar to the process of starting a nation, all the guidelines for governing justly can be found in the first five books of the Bible, authored by Moses. These governing principles are reiterated across thousands of verses throughout the Old and New Testaments. Therefore, our challenge is to identify these verses and extract the governing principles that Israel initially embraced to live out their national covenant in the civil arena.

To clarify, we're not discussing the ceremonial law, nor are we suggesting that all the specific laws and punishments given to Israel should be applied in America or any other nation. We focus solely on the principles that guarantee liberty and civil justice for everyone residing in a specific community or nation.

We will distill God's guidelines for just governance into seven principles applicable not only to civil governments but also to households. These principles serve as a blueprint that any home, community, or nation worldwide seeking to honor God can adopt to receive His blessings.

To delve into the first principle, we will revisit the earlier section on how to start a nation. In that context, we learned that governments are formed through a mutual covenant, founded on the free consent of the people. Moreover, God provided the Israelites with seven annual feasts designed to remind them of all that God had accomplished for them and why they should stay dedicated to their national covenant. Building on this understanding, we can identify the first principle for governing a nation that honors God:

1. Governments are established through a mutual covenant by the free consent of the people, to which they recommit annually.

Once the people had agreed to follow God in return for His blessings, God entrusted Moses with the Ten Commandments, which serve as a concise summary of the Moral Law. This is detailed in Exodus 20, and the significance of obeying God's commandments is emphasized throughout the rest of the Bible:

> And God spoke all these words: "I am the LORD your God, who brought you out of Egypt, out of the land of slavery. You shall have no other gods before me." (Exod. 20:1–3)

> Whoever has my commands and keeps them is the one who loves me. The one who loves me will be loved by my Father, and I too will love them and show myself to them. (John 14:21)

Understanding the importance of the Moral Law and striving to live by it cannot be emphasized enough. I delve into greater detail in my first book, but here's a summary of how the Moral Law should guide our lives:

- First, the Moral Law helps us understand the holiness of God.
- Second, it reveals our need for a savior, as we cannot keep the law perfectly at all times.
- Third, once a person embraces faith in Christ, the Moral Law directs how to lead a life that honors God.
- Fourth, the Moral Law provides the framework for all legitimate lawmaking.

From this, we arrive at the second principle when establishing a nation that honors God:

2. Governments must embrace God's Moral Law as the standard to guide personal behavior and all lawmaking.

Next, in Exodus 18, we observe how God worked through Moses's father-in-law, Jethro, to delegate authority for resolving civil disputes among the people:

> But select capable men from all the people—men who fear God, trustworthy men who hate dishonest gain—and appoint them as officials over thousands, hundreds, fifties, and tens. Have them serve as judges for the people at all times ... (Exod. 18:21–22)

Moses repeated this process of appointing officials to manage governance in his final book, Deuteronomy 16:

Appoint judges and officials for each of your tribes in every town the LORD your God is giving you, and they shall judge the people fairly. Do not pervert justice or show partiality. Do not accept a bribe, for a bribe blinds the eyes of the wise and twists the words of the innocent. Follow justice and justice alone, so that you may live and possess the land the LORD your God is giving you. (Deut. 16:18–20)

From these verses, we see the third principle when establishing a God-honoring nation:

3. Representative government consists of elected officials who promise to govern by God's Moral Law.

The next question concerning government revolves around identifying the essential rights of the people that the government is duty-bound to safeguard. Protecting these rights, particularly a person's right to life, constitutes the primary purpose behind establishing civil government, making it of utmost importance to God. The Bible makes many references to these rights:

Woe to those who make unjust laws, to those who issue oppressive decrees, to deprive the poor of their rights and withhold justice from the oppressed of my people, making widows their prey and robbing the fatherless. (Isa. 10:1–2)

Speak up for those who cannot speak for themselves, for the rights of all who are destitute. Speak up and judge fairly; defend the rights of the poor and needy. (Prov. 31:8–9)

According to Noah Webster's 1828 dictionary, the founding generation recognized the unbreakable link between an individual's rights and the Moral Law, which encompasses every aspect of personal life:

Right (noun, 13 definitions listed) – (1) Conformity to the will of God or to his law, the perfect standard of truth and justice; (10) Just claim; Immunity; privilege. All men have a right to the secure enjoyment of life, personal safety, liberty and property. We deem the right of trial by jury invaluable, particularly in the case of crimes. Rights are natural, civil, political, religious, personal, and public.[8]

James Otis, a notable Boston lawyer and representative in the Massachusetts General Court during the 1760s, presented his argument in February of 1761:

There must be in every instance, a higher authority, viz. God. Should an act of parliament be against any of his natural laws, which are immutably true, their declaration would be contrary to eternal truth, equity, and justice, and consequently void.[9]

From these verses we see the fourth principle when establishing a God-honoring nation, which the founding generation readily recognized:

4. Legitimate rights of individuals must conform to the Moral Law.

The fundamental role of any governing authority is to prevent and restrain evil as it emerges in the form of crimes against law-abiding citizens. The Bible unequivocally emphasizes the importance of punishing wrongdoers as a means to deter future violence (Deut. 17:12–13; Eccles. 8:11), with the severity of punishment corresponding to the gravity of the offense:

> If people are fighting and hit a pregnant woman and she gives birth prematurely but there is no serious injury, the offender must be fined whatever the woman's husband demands and the court allows. But if there is serious injury, you are to take life for life, eye for eye, tooth for tooth, hand for hand, foot for foot, burn for burn, wound for wound, bruise for bruise. (Exod. 21:22–25)

> Anyone who takes the life of a human being is to be put to death. Anyone who takes the life of someone's animal must make restitution—life for life. Anyone who injures their neighbor is to be injured in the same manner: fracture for fracture, eye for eye, tooth for tooth. The one who has inflicted the injury must suffer the same injury.

Whoever kills an animal must make restitution, but whoever kills a human being is to be put to death. You are to
have the same law for the foreigner and the native-born. I
am the LORD your God. (Lev. 24:17–22)

This means the fifth principle when establishing a God-honoring nation is the following:

5. Laws passed must be enforced through equal justice, where punishment matches the level of the crime.

One of the most significant challenges when living in a community with others is granting them the freedom to express themselves, even when their views differ from yours. This freedom
to voice opinions is what we define as liberty. Throughout the
Bible, there are numerous verses in which God invites mankind to contemplate their beliefs and exercise their freedom to
choose to follow Him:

- We see this in Genesis 2:15–17, where God explains to
  Adam and Eve that they are not to eat from the tree of
  knowledge of good and evil, but He allows them to consider and choose what they will do.
- We see it in Isaiah 1, where God says, "Come, let us reason," explaining the option of salvation where their sins
  can be "white as snow."
- In Psalms 81, God affirms His pleading for His people to
  follow Him, but they would not listen; they would not
  choose to submit to Him.

- In Matthew 23:37, Jesus is lamenting how He has longed to gather their children together as a hen gathers her chicks, but they refused because they had the liberty to do so.
- Finally, in Revelation 20:7–8, after years of Christ reigning while Satan is bound, "Satan will be released from his prison and will go out to deceive the nations in the four corners of the earth." This will lead to the final battle between good and evil, which will happen because God will allow those living at that time the liberty to form their own opinion and choose whom they will follow.

Liberty can also pertain to civil matters involving one's property, including one's physical body.* Verses such as the ones below affirm that God expects people to have their civil liberties safeguarded as well:

You shall not steal. (Exod. 20:15)

Cursed is anyone who moves their neighbor's boundary stone. (Deut. 27:17)

---

* The Progressive position toward COVID-19 vaccines was that citizens could be forced to take the vaccine despite the concerns a person might have with the way in which the vaccine was developed and tested (using aborted fetal cells) or because of the unknown potential adverse effects. These are examples of religious and civil liberties critical to the founding of America. Importantly, if a person cannot have a say in what is injected in their bodies (civil liberty), what good are property rights?

There are those who move boundary stones; they pasture flocks they have stolen. (Job 24:2)

He [Jesus] said to them, "But now if you have a purse, take it, and also a bag; and if you don't have a sword, sell your cloak and buy one." (Luke 22:36)

In Abraham Lincoln's Gettysburg Address, he noted that America was "conceived in liberty," a quality not commonly held in such high regard by nations. Living in a country where people strongly disagree with its founding principles, as in America, can present challenges. While it remains crucial to emphasize the significance of liberty, loyal and patriotic citizens must also articulate and defend American values to ensure the strength and ongoing vitality of the nation while preserving this essential principle from its founding.

This means the sixth principle when establishing a God-honoring nation is as follows:

6. Liberty is to be extended to all, regardless of religious belief.

Lastly, we see a constant theme in the Old and New Testaments of passing on all Moses taught the Israelites to the next generation:

> Only be careful and watch yourselves closely so that you do not forget the things your eyes have seen or let them fade from your heart as long as you live. Teach them to

your children and to their children after them. (Deut. 4:9–10)

Fathers . . . bring them up in the training and instruction of the Lord. (Eph. 6:4)

The seventh and final principle when establishing a God-honoring nation is the following:

7. The community, especially the next generation, needs to be educated on these principles.

These seven principles for governing justly that we learn from Israel are meant to be adopted by all other nations of the world. Nations that earnestly commit to establishing a God-honoring nation through a covenant and follow these governing principles can generally expect to be blessed by God.

A crucial point of clarification relates to these seven principles, specifically concerning the Moral Law and the Israelites' covenant in Exodus 19–24 when Moses presented the Moral Law engraved on two stone tablets. Many theologians describe this scene as follows: "God presented the Moral Law, saying that if you keep these commands, I will bless you, but if you do not, I will curse you." They assert that the implication was that God would only bless them if they ALL kept the commands perfectly, which, of course, was impossible. Consequently, the Israelites were doomed to failure and judgment, which they experienced. However, this interpretation is inaccurate for what transpired in Exodus 19–24.

This was not a covenant contingent on the Israelites' flawless adherence to living according to the Moral Law. Instead, it was a national governing covenant mediated by Moses, in which the Israelites committed to striving to live by the Moral Law as the standard, using the governing structure and decrees outlined by Moses. The evidence supporting this interpretation is clear first from the many ways God explained that the Israelites were to atone for sin, as described in the book of Leviticus. Clearly, God expected sinful behavior to be ongoing. Evidence can also be found in the principle of securing justice, where the punishment was meant to correspond with the severity of the crime (principle #5). This principle suggests that God acknowledged sinful behavior would occur in the civil arena, not that individual moral perfection would be achieved. When sin did occur in the civil arena, God expected Israel's leaders to secure justice for the victim.

A practical example of this occurred during the most prosperous period of Israel, which was under King Solomon's rule. There was a case in which two women claimed the same baby as their own, leading to a serious and difficult civil dispute that eventually reached Solomon. He ordered the living baby to be cut in half, but the real mother objected, making it evident to all who the true mother was (1 Kings 3:16-28). During this period, God clearly blessed Israel; however, when Solomon later allowed the worship of other gods, he disrespected Israel's national covenant. As a result, God withdrew His blessing, just as He did with other poor leaders throughout history.

Keeping the Ten Commandments perfectly is impossible for anyone. However, striving to live peacefully with our neighbors by applying biblical principles to establish a nation and govern it justly is entirely feasible. It is akin to the possibility of maintaining a healthy marriage between two imperfect individuals, raising godly and productive yet flawed children, and living within one's financial means. God provides principles in the Bible to succeed in all these areas if one is willing to learn and commit to applying these principles. Just as Israel was capable of governing according to its national covenant when its leaders were committed to it, all nations worldwide can adopt these same governing principles and experience God's blessings when they sincerely committed to doing so.

SUMMARY

We have covered a lot in answering this first question, "What does God expect from the nations?" Yet it is not terribly complicated:

1. **God's Expectations for Nations**: God desires nations to be *fruitful, increase in number, fill the earth,* and *govern justly.*

2. **Biblical Blueprint to Start a Nation**: God desires new nations to formally recognize Him through a mutual covenant agreed to by the free consent of the people involved. He has a simple template for how to start a nation, one that is the same for starting a marriage and family. God wants those entering into the covenant to

acknowledge Him and relevant principles given the content of the covenant, *appeal* to Him for His help to see the covenant through, *commit* based on the legal customs of the culture, and *declare* it publicly.

3. **Biblical Principles for Governing Justly**: God demands that nations govern justly. He provides seven principles on how to do this:

   - Governments are established and maintained through a mutual covenant by the free consent of the people, reaffirmed annually.
   - Governments are to embrace God's Moral Law as the standard to guide personal behavior and lawmaking.
   - Representative government is essential, with elected officials promising to govern in accordance with God's Moral Law.
   - Legitimate rights of individuals must align with the Moral Law, including life, liberty, and the pursuit of happiness, which the founders meant as pursuing God as one's conscience dictates.
   - Laws passed must be enforced through equal and impartial justice, with punishments matching the level of the crime.
   - Liberty should be extended to all, regardless of religious belief.
   - The community should be educated on these principles to enable everyone to live peacefully with their neighbors. This allows citizens to love their neighbor, even those with a different faith.

Israel received this information and was entrusted with the task of sharing it with the world's nations. God intended for all nations to understand and honor Him in their ways of living and governing. Any nation could receive God's blessings by comprehending and embracing these principles. This objective is consistently reiterated in both the Old and New Testaments:

> Therefore, you kings, be wise; be warned, you rulers of the earth. Serve the LORD with fear and celebrate his rule with trembling. Kiss his son, or he will be angry and your way will lead to your destruction, for his wrath can flare up in a moment. Blessed are all who take refuge in him. (Ps. 2:10–12)

> Blessed is the nation whose God is the LORD, the people he chose for his inheritance. From heaven the LORD looks down and sees all mankind; from his dwelling place he watches all who live on earth—he who forms the hearts of all, who considers everything they do. (Ps. 33:12–15)

> Praise the LORD from the earth, you great sea creatures and all ocean depths, lightning and hail, snow and clouds, stormy winds that do his bidding, you mountains and all hills, fruit trees and all cedars, wild animals and all cattle, small creatures and flying birds, kings of the earth and all nations, you princes and all rulers on earth, young men and women, old men and children. Let them praise the

name of the LORD, for his name alone is exalted; his splendor is above the earth and the heavens. (Ps. 148:7–13)

From one man he made all the nations, that they should inhabit the whole earth; and he marked out their appointed times in history and the boundaries of their lands. God did this so that they would seek him and perhaps reach out for him and find him, though he is not far from any one of us. (Acts 17:26–27)

The Bible offers timeless guidance to all who seek to honor God in their lives, including how they interact within their communities and with other nations. The question that persists to this day is: How have nations fared in adhering to these principles? The answer hinges on those who step forward to lead in the civil arena. This topic will be explored in the next chapter.

CHAPTER 2

GOD'S CIVIC EXPECTATIONS OF INDIVIDUALS

Once we grasp the biblical principles for starting a nation and governing it justly, the pivotal question arises: Who will step forward and take up the responsibility to apply these principles to establish a just civil authority?

In the latter half of the twentieth century, the evangelical establishment prioritized missions as the paramount activity while downplaying the importance of citizenship. According to their perspective, a spiritually mature Christian focuses solely on sharing the gospel. Contrary to this view, anyone suggesting that political engagement is also an important part of the Christian faith is often labeled as misguided or spiritually immature. They are accused of working against the Great Commission, which aims to evangelize the lost.

In this chapter, I will argue that the exact opposite is true.

WHO IS RESPONSIBLE?

A critical question emerges after recognizing biblical guidelines for establishing a just civil authority for the nations that would form after Noah: Who does God expect to step forward to establish and uphold justice? This question holds particular relevance in today's context, where many within the evangelical church advocate for Christians simply submitting to and praying for civil authorities.

To explore this further, we can divide the population into several groups to contemplate who God might expect to fulfill this citizenship duty:

Group 1: Is it those who do not know God or the Bible?

Is it reasonable to assume that this group, with little to no knowledge about how to ensure justice, can meet God's expectations in this regard? While it's possible for someone who doesn't know God to be an effective civil leader and approximate the dispensation of justice as God intends, is it this person who God would expect to govern, a person who lacks biblical knowledge of Him and access to His word?

Group 2: Is it those who reject God and the Bible?

It should be evident that God is not looking to this group, which rejects Him, to establish and uphold justice as described in the Bible.

Group 3: Is it those who acknowledge there is a God, or maybe a new believer, but do not know their Bible?

There is a higher likelihood that this group would govern justly as they acquire more knowledge if they were growing in their faith and reading their Bible. However, is this God's first choice when it comes to governing justly?

Group 4: Is it those who know God and generally read their Bible regularly, especially if they have talent and/or the spiritual gift of leadership or administration?

It appears evident that in this modern age, Christian believers would be the most qualified group to understand what God expects in this area and be capable of dispensing justice fairly to all, provided they have been properly taught how to do this.

It seems clear that Genesis 9:5–6 represents God's initial call to active citizenship for all people throughout history and that this call is directed at those who claim to follow Him. This call happened before God called Abraham and the formation of Israel. This call entails governing justly as God's servants, acting for the collective good by defending individual rights. It seems very apparent that today this responsibility is bestowed upon Christians. It is *our duty*.

This context is crucial when examining New Testament verses like Romans 13, which suggests that the call to submission in Romans 13 is contingent on the presence of a *just civil authority* that *rewards* those who do good and *punishes* those who commit evil acts:

> For rulers hold no terror for those who do right, but *for those who do wrong.* Do you want to be free from fear of the one in authority? Then *do what is right and you will be commended.* For the one in authority is God's servant for your good. But *if you do wrong, be afraid,* for rulers do not bear the sword for no reason. They are God's servants, *agents of wrath to bring punishment on the wrongdoer.* (Rom. 13:3–4)

This passage affirms the biblical role of a just civil authority, which is to commend those who do good and punish wrongdoers. Therefore, Romans 13 reinforces the principles of a just civil authority originally outlined in Genesis 9 rather than introducing a new principle that mandates unconditional submission to the governing authority.

Why God Desires Believers to Step Forward to Lead

Chapter 1 discussed God's aspirations for nations: to prosper, multiply, inhabit the earth, and uphold justice. However, there's another crucial reason why God seeks to establish liberty and justice for all. We see the answer in what Moses conveys to the Israelites in Deuteronomy 4:

See, I have taught you decrees and laws as the LORD my God commanded me, so that you may follow them in the land you are entering to take possession of it. Observe them carefully, for this will show your wisdom and understanding to the nations, who will hear about all these decrees and say, "Surely this great nation is a wise and understanding people." What other nation is so great as to have their gods near them the way the LORD our God is near us whenever we pray to him? And what other nation is so great as to have such righteous decrees and laws as this body of laws I am setting before you today? (Deut. 4:5–8)

In the Old Testament, governing justly served as God's evangelistic strategy. We discover the effectiveness of this strategy through the visit of the Queen of Sheba, who came to test Solomon with numerous questions. In the end, her visit confirmed the success of this approach:

The report I heard in my own country about your achievements and your wisdom is true. But I did not believe these things until I came and saw with my own eyes. Indeed, not even half was told me; in wisdom and wealth you have far exceeded the report I heard. How happy your people must be! How happy your officials, who continually stand before you and hear your wisdom! Praise be to the LORD your God, who has delighted in you and placed you on the throne of Israel. Because of the LORD's eternal love for

Israel, he has made you king to maintain justice and righteousness. (1 Kings 10:6–9)

One might wonder if this was a genuine conversion, but Jesus answers this question when the Pharisees came to him asking for a sign:

A wicked and adulterous generation asks for a sign! But none will be given it except the sign of the prophet Jonah. For as Jonah was three days and three nights in the belly of a huge fish, so the Son of Man will be three days and three nights in the heart of the earth. The men of Nineveh will stand up at the judgment with this generation and condemn it; for they repented at the preaching of Jonah, and now something greater than Jonah is here. The Queen of the South will rise at the judgment with this generation and condemn it; for she came from the ends of the earth to listen to Solomon's wisdom, and now something greater than Solomon is here. (Matt. 12:39–42)

This encounter in the gospels reveals that the Queen of Sheba experienced a genuine conversion. By her admission, the key factor contributing to her conversion was witnessing the blessings bestowed upon Israel because of Solomon's just and righteous governance as a king. This aligns precisely with Moses's indication of the desired outcome for surrounding nations if Israel remained faithful in governing justly.

In the New Testament, we find additional guidance regarding the role of nations and Christians in God's evangelistic plan. Paul, during his ministry to the Gentile nations, affirmed the evangelistic role of nations as laid out in Genesis 9:1-7 and Deuteronomy 4:5-8:

> The God who made the world and everything in it is the Lord of heaven and earth and does not live in temples built by human hands. And he is not served by human hands, as if he needed anything. Rather, he himself gives everyone life and breath and everything else. From one man he made all the nations, that they should inhabit the whole earth; and he marked out their appointed times in history and the boundaries of their lands. God did this so that they would seek him and perhaps reach out for him and find him . . . (Acts 17:24–27)

In this passage, Paul reflects on God's plan for the nations, clarified after the flood. God intended for nations to emerge, populate the world, and govern justly, enabling their citizens to "seek Him and perhaps find Him." Paul later affirms God's desire that people live peaceful and quiet lives where they can consider following God and instructs his protégé, Timothy, that this requires praying for our civil leaders:

> I urge, then, first of all, that petitions, prayers, intercession and thanksgiving be made for all people—for kings and

all those in authority, that we may live peaceful and quiet lives in all godliness and holiness. This is good, and pleases God our Savior, who wants all people to be saved and to come to a knowledge of the truth. (1 Tim. 2:1–4)

Put simply, a just civil government is a crucial requirement for leading peaceful and godly lives in a society that fosters fellowship with God and spreading the gospel. This aligns perfectly with the teachings about civil government in the Old Testament.

To emphasize the significance of putting faith into action in the civil arena, the writer of Hebrews highlights administering justice as the driving force behind numerous Old Testament figures receiving the promises made to them:

And what more shall I say? I do not have time to tell about Gideon, Barak, Samson and Jephthah, about David and Samuel and the prophets, who through faith conquered kingdoms, administered justice, and gained what was promised ... (Heb. 11:32–33)

In 2 Corinthians, Paul identifies virtues that should come as Christians mature in their faith, including the desire to secure justice:

Godly sorrow brings repentance that leads to salvation and leaves no regret, but worldly sorrow brings death. See what this godly sorrow has produced in you: what earnestness, what eagerness to clear yourselves what indignation, what alarm, what longing, what concern, *what readiness to see justice done.* (2 Cor. 7:10–11)

Lastly, Paul underscores the role of the Holy Spirit in cultivating the virtues necessary for Christians to live in harmony with God and their neighbors. This empowerment uniquely equips Christians to contribute even more effectively to the establishment of a just society with law and order:

But the fruit of the Spirit is love, joy, peace, forbearance, kindness, goodness, faithfulness, gentleness and self-control; against such things there is no law. (Gal. 5:22–23)

With the Holy Spirit as our guide and an expanding grasp of Scripture, believers can serve as God's instruments for promoting justice in their communities and nations. We have easy access to God's blueprint for living out our Christian faith with growing effectiveness. Supported by the Holy Spirit, our righteous conduct guides us to reject ungodliness and worldly desires, leading us to lead self-controlled, upright, and godly lives in the present age (Titus 2:12).

When Christians align their personal lives with God's design, they resemble Solomon's Israel, drawing others into their circle, much like the Queen of Sheba. In doing so, we adopt God's Old Testament evangelism strategy as our own. As individuals, we become a city on a hill, a beacon for the gospel.

Given all this, how should Christians apply the Great Commission given in the gospel of Matthew? For many sincere

Christians living today, the pivotal passage that appears crucial to steering our daily priorities is found in Matthew 28:18–20. This is where Jesus instructs the disciples to share the gospel with the nations of the world:

> Then Jesus came to them and said, "All authority in heaven and on earth has been given to me. Therefore go and make disciples of all nations, baptizing them in the name of the Father and of the Son and of the Holy Spirit, and teaching them to obey everything I have commanded you. And surely I am with you always, to the very end of the age." (Matt. 28:18–20)

Given all we have explored regarding civil government in the Old Testament, what additional insights might we glean from this passage?

If we examine this verse solely from a New Testament perspective, it might appear that Jesus is providing fresh directives. However, this is not the case. First, observe the emphasis on nations, which is not a new concept; it is merely a reaffirmation of what we find in the Old Testament:

> I will praise you, LORD, among the nations; I will sing of you among the peoples. (Ps. 108:3)

> Praise the LORD, all you nations; extol him, all you peoples. For great is his love toward us, and the faithfulness of the LORD endures forever. (Ps. 117:1–2)

Second, Jesus instructs the disciples to teach new believers everything He has commanded them. This encompasses the Old Testament and principles for establishing a just civil authority. Nothing in Jesus's teachings implies that the instructions in the Old Testament regarding civil government have become irrelevant. Moreover, other New Testament writers support the significance of civil government, as seen in passages like Romans 13 and 1 Timothy 2. So, what is Jesus conveying with the Great Commission in Matthew 28?

God's intention to draw nations closer to Himself remains constant, but His approach to evangelism has evolved. A significant aspect of God's evangelistic strategy for Israel was for them to inhabit the land He had granted them. God recognized the importance of location, as He had provided Israel with a unique geographical position as a natural land bridge connecting major continents. In the ancient world, travelers inevitably passed through Israel, where they could witness its distinct governance structure and experience the divine blessings upon the nation. To accomplish this, Israel was to *stay* in that location given that it was literally the crossroads of civilization.

The Queen of Sheba serves as an example; she had heard about Israel's blessings and traveled a considerable distance to witness them firsthand (like a modern-day *seeker*). In doing so, she encountered God.

God's evangelistic strategy changed with the arrival of Jesus, who bore the world's sin and ushered in the New Covenant (Luke 22:20; 1 Cor. 11:25). Through Jesus's crucifixion and resurrection, all who believe in Him had their sins forgiven and were reconciled to God. The Old Testament sacrifices, which served as a temporary sin covering, were rendered obsolete, and anyone, regardless of their location, could now have direct access to God through His Son by accepting Him as their savior.

With Christ's resurrection, God's plan for evangelism entered a new phase. The disciples, who were initially Jews, were no longer instructed to STAY in the land God had given Israel and govern justly as the primary means of revealing God to the world. Instead, with the advent of the gospel centered on the risen Christ and a New Covenant for the world, Jesus's disciples were commissioned to GO and share the gospel with all the nations across the globe. The purpose of civil government, which is to establish law and order to facilitate every individual's personal faith journey, remained unchanged. This underscores the critical importance of establishing a just civil authority and why people of faith have always carried the responsibility of stepping forward to lead in this area.

WHAT TAKES PRIORITY?

The contemporary evangelical church emphasizes that every facet of the Christian life should be seen through the lens of evangelism. In simpler terms, evangelism precedes everything else; it is the unmistakable priority for the serious Christian. However, this perspective seems inconsistent with the lessons from the 1,500-year period before the Flood. During those generations, people had direct access to Adam and Eve and their story; yet society ultimately deteriorated into violence, prompting God to intervene with a devastating flood that wiped out mankind except for Noah and his family.

The lesson we should draw from this era is that without a just civil authority, a society will descend into chaos and tyranny—it is just a matter of time. Recent history confirms this to be true (North Korea, Iran, Afghanistan, Venezuela, and even major, Progressive-run US cities with high crime rates). God, desiring a fruitful and peaceful existence for us (as mentioned in Gen. 9:1 and 1 Tim. 2:2), established the institution of civil government to prevent this chaos and foster a just, enduring, stable society. Therefore, to the extent possible, creating and maintaining a just and civil society should be the foremost priority for existing Christians in their respective communities and nations.

Let's consider a straightforward example: maintaining law and order within a household with numerous children. When children engage in a dispute leading to a brawl, should the parent resolve the situation by simply saying, "Jesus loves you and has a wonderful plan for your life"? Or should they step in to break up the fight?* Answer: they should break up the fight.

Similar to the analogy between establishing a national covenant and governing justly, or to establishing a marriage covenant and ensuring justice within the home, the paramount goal is to create an environment where everyone can coexist harmoniously whether they believe in God or not. This objective

---

* We have four children and experienced this firsthand on more than one occasion.

becomes especially crucial when family members may have conflicts or disagreements with each other.

While it is essential for Christians to always be ready to share the gospel (1 Pet. 3:15), it is equally crucial to understand that *concentrating on establishing justice within their sphere of influence takes priority*. This lays the groundwork for evangelistic conversations just as it did in the days of Solomon. The key point is recognizing how crucial it is for Christians to prioritize justice, as it will enable evangelism.

SCOPE OF GOVERNMENT: IMPOSE RIGHTEOUSNESS OR EXTEND LIBERTY?

A common point of debate among Christians during the Church Age has been the scope of responsibility for the civil authority.* Specifically, should the government impose certain Christian doctrines on the citizenry beyond the Moral Law, even though citizens do not embrace the Christian faith?†

Both religious and civil leaders claiming to represent God have been guilty of imposing certain doctrinal positions and of persecuting dissenters during the Church Age, even to the extent of torture and killings. These different positions were driven in large part by different views on the manner and time

---

* The Church Age is the time since the resurrection of Christ to today, about two thousand years.

† The basics of the Moral Law that apply to all are protection of life and property. We will talk more about the Moral Law in the next chapter.

when Jesus would return and how he would establish his kingdom, which many Bible verses describe. A detailed explanation of these different views and how they evolved during the Church Age is beyond the scope of this book. However, we can at least define the different governing positions and compare them to the point of view that will be explained in the remainder of this book.

Finding a simple explanation of the different positions on the proper role of civil government and the church turned out to be very difficult. Serendipitously, years ago a friend gave me *Christian Theology of Public Policy* by John M. Cobin. In his book Cobin provides a table explaining the various positions, which I include and expand upon in Table 2.1.

While there are a lot of variations within these different positions, I will explain the basic differences that traditionally distinguish these views from one another and the resulting actions of the civil authority. I fully recognize many variations within these views exist that this simple explanation will not address; however, I believe this is a good model to understand how people have generally viewed the role of civil government throughout the Church Age.

Cobin calls out two general interpretive approaches to this question. In the first, the church or state ruler imposes Christianity on the citizenry to varying degrees, claiming a biblical or divine right to do so. In this view, Jesus reigns on earth through the church or through the state ruler as "established by God" (a way to interpret Rom. 13). Some holding this view believe that not only the civil code should be imposed but also the penalties God prescribed for the Israelites, including the death penalty

TABLE 2.1

Two Basic Approaches	Integrated Authority of State and God's Law Imposing Biblical Laws and Penalties		Two-Kingdom View, with God's Kingdom Preeminent and the Moral Law as the Legal Standard	
Different Positions	*State Authority:* Divine Right of Kings	*Religious Authority:* Post-Millennialism Theonomy, Reconstruction, Christian Nationalism	*Separate and Submissive:* Support and Pray for Civil Leaders	*Separate and Responsible To Establish Civil Government:* Protect Liberty and Justice for All
Different Viewpoints Regarding Church and Government	Impose God's will as discerned by the King.	Church imposes doctrinal positions through a state-sponsored Church. Church imposes Old Testament law through the king.	Limited church involvement in civil government. Focus on building God's heavenly Kingdom through evangelism.	View government as an institution given by God to enable nations to honor God by securing justice. The Church should be active in training civil leaders and be the moral conscience for society, including government officials.

| Kingdom Perspective | King/ruler not subject to earthly laws given that they are ordained by God.[10] The King or Queen may impose what he or she feels is best. | Government to be used to usher in God's Kingdom by imposing Christianity on the citizenry.[11] | See earthly kingdoms as hopelessly corrupt and a distraction to the Great Commission. See themselves as "citizens of another kingdom," with that heavenly kingdom being the primary focus of Christians. | Dual citizenship, but ultimate allegiance to God's Kingdom, which is yet to fully come.[*] Recognize the challenge of corrupt government but see government as a blessing from God and believe He expects us to do our best to apply biblical principles of liberty, rights, and justice in civil government. |

* Luke 22:29–30; John 14:2; Acts 22:22–29; Eph. 2:9; Phil. 3:20–21; Heb. 13:14; 1 Pet. 1:4; Rev. 21:2, 27, 22:3–5.

(by stoning) for adultery, incest, and homosexuality.[12] During the Church Age, civil leaders have often claimed a divine right to impose laws on their citizens as they see fit—often viewing themselves as above the law. The drafting of the Magna Carta by barons living in Runnymede in 1215 and the signing of it by King John is the classic example of citizens challenging the king's supposedly limitless power. The American founders were essentially claiming the same problem with King George when they listed twenty-seven ways in the Declaration of Independence of how the king had exceeded his God-given authority and governed unjustly. The common thread in these positions is an imposition of what the civil leader or state-sponsored church believes is best. This often leads to the infringement of rights at best and persecution and martyrdom at worst.

The second view is very different in that it recognizes there are two kingdoms: God's Kingdom in heaven where he is ruling now and earthly kingdoms where God allows mankind to govern using principles laid out in the Old Testament. This two-kingdom view believes that Jesus reigning on earth is a future event.* It has two subviews: one where the church is responsible *to* civil government and is more passively involved (SEPARATE AND SUBMISSIVE), and the other where the church is responsible *for* civil government (SEPARATE AND RESPONSI-BLE). Importantly, this SEPARATE AND RESPONSIBLE view, also seeking to apply biblical principles of civil justice, differs from

---

* Theologians debate the details of when and how Jesus will reign in the future, but these differences do not materially change the resulting view that God appoints civil governments as part of this "two-kingdom" view.

the first two views in that it embraces liberty as the foundational principle. This difference is what prohibits the persecution by state or church leaders of dissenters (religious or not) that has been prevalent during much of the Church Age. Furthermore, it recognizes the need for a voluntary covenant made through the consent of the people to establish a legitimate governing body with the power needed to govern justly.

This SEPARATE AND RESPONSIBLE view is what motivated the American founders. They recognized the importance of a covenant agreed to by the mutual consent of the people (liberty). They also understood that violating a person's liberty led to persecution, and they believed God wants everyone to make his or her own choice regarding faith. Thomas Jefferson articulated this well in his Virginia Statute for Religious Freedom (1786):

> Whereas, Almighty God hath created the mind free; That all attempts to influence it by temporal punishments or burthens, or by civil incapacitations tend only to beget habits of hypocrisy and meanness, and therefore are a departure from the plan of the holy author of our religion, who being Lord, both of body and mind yet chose not to propagate it by coercions on either, as was in his Almighty power to do, That the impious presumption of legislators and rulers, civil as well as ecclesiastical, who, being themselves but fallible and uninspired men have assumed dominion over the faith of others, setting up their own

opinions and modes of thinking as the only true and infallible, and as such endeavoring to impose them on others, hath established and maintained false religions over the greatest part of the world and through all time.*[13]

The SEPARATE AND SUBMISSIVE view is the view held by the majority of today's evangelical churches, justifying a passive and optional approach to citizenship. The SEPARATE AND RESPONSIBLE view recognizes Christians are the ones God expects to step forward and lead, as we are the ones who are committed to living our lives according to the principles given to us in the Bible. This view also holds that, while Christians should be actively leading in the civil arena based on the parameters of the covenant, individual liberty must always be respected. This SEPARATE AND RESPONSIBLE view is the view we are promoting in this book.

---

* Modern historians often cite passages like this to promote the idea that Jefferson was antichurch, but this is not the case. When looking at all of what he wrote over his life, what is clear is that he did not approve of state-sanctioned churches that subsidized their clergy. He found it especially bad when this clergy forced or imposed their beliefs on others yet were not living out moral principles clearly taught by Jesus himself. He fought to disestablish the state church in Virginia for this reason, instead promoting the idea that churches should directly pay for their pastors based on a voluntary congregation. This is the model most churches in America follow today—paying for their clergy directly.

SUMMARY

In this chapter, we have not only clarified that every Christian must step forward and apply biblical principles to starting a community or nation and governing justly, but we have also emphasized how central this is to God's strategy for evangelism. It sets the stage for sharing the gospel and provides an opportunity to illustrate how the Judeo-Christian faith uniquely fosters peaceful societies, promoting liberty and justice for all. Furthermore, it is crucial to recognize that this citizenship duty is not optional; instead, it holds paramount importance for individuals of faith within their families, communities, and the nations where they reside.

CHAPTER 3

RESPONSIBILITY OF CHRISTIANS WHEN BEING GOVERNED JUSTLY

In previous chapters, we have explored the responsibility Christians bear in establishing and governing communities and nations in a way that aligns with God's principles. However, in this chapter, we shift our focus to the perspective of the citizen. Regardless of whether civil leaders are Christians, unbelievers, or radicals, the central question we will address is this: how should citizens, particularly Christians, respond when they are governed justly? It is also essential to clarify what it means to govern justly and what it entails.

In this chapter, we will outline this concept while considering the critical institutions God ordained to enable humanity to lead productive, fulfilling lives while individually going on their own faith journeys.

CHRISTIAN RESPONSE TO BEING GOVERNED JUSTLY

Among all the questions concerning civil government, the modern evangelical establishment is quite clear on this one. It is a two-part answer, with the first part being that all citizens should submit to their governing authorities when those authorities govern justly. This principle is evident in passages like Romans 13 and 1 Peter 2:

> Let everyone be subject to the governing authorities, for there is no authority except that which God has established. The authorities that exist have been established by God. Consequently, whoever rebels against the authority is rebelling against what God has instituted, and those who do so will bring judgment on themselves. For rulers hold no terror for those who do right, but for those who do wrong. Do you want to be free from fear of the one in authority? Then do what is right and you will be commended. For the one in authority is God's servant for your good. But if you do wrong, be afraid, for rulers do not bear the sword for no reason. They are God's servants, agents of wrath to bring punishment on the wrongdoer. Therefore, it is necessary to submit to the authorities, not only because of possible punishment but also as a matter of conscience. (Rom. 13:1–5)

> Submit yourselves for the Lord's sake to every human authority: whether to the emperor, as the supreme

authority, or to governors, who are sent by him to punish those who do wrong and to commend those who do right. For it is God's will that by doing good you should silence the ignorant talk of foolish people. Live as free people, but do not use your freedom as a cover-up for evil; live as God's slaves. Show proper respect to everyone, love the family of believers, fear God, honor the emperor. (1 Pet. 2:13–17)

These passages confirm that God expects civil leaders to commend those who do good and punish those who break the law. When this occurs, all citizens must submit to the laws they are enacting.

The second part of the answer is that Christians are to pray for their civil leaders, asking God to grant them wisdom for wise governance. This is crucial because it is through wise civil leaders that we can live in peace, pursuing God as our individual conscience dictates. This principle is affirmed in the New Testament in 1 Timothy 2:

I urge, then, first of all, that petitions, prayers, intercession and thanksgiving be made for all people—for kings and all those in authority, that we may live peaceful and quiet lives in all godliness and holiness. This is good, and pleases God our Savior, who wants all people to be saved and to come to a knowledge of the truth. (1 Tim. 2:1–4)

Therefore, the Christian response when the civil authority is governing justly is to submit to it and pray for it. This leads to the next question: what does it look like to govern justly? How can one recognize being governed justly based on what they observe and experience?

WHAT GOVERNING JUSTLY LOOKS LIKE

Evaluating whether a civil authority is governing justly hinges on two key factors: their adherence to the Moral Law and their respect for the institutions established by God for humanity.

As discussed in earlier chapters, the Moral Law forms the cornerstone of our relationship with God, indicating of His standard of righteousness and highlighting our inability to meet that standard. Consequently, it underscores our status as sinners in need of salvation to avoid eternal separation from God. Our salvation is exclusively achievable through Jesus's sacrificial death on the cross, where He paid the sin debt for all of humanity. Upon accepting Jesus as our Lord, we embark on a lifelong journey to grow more like Him, essentially learning to align our lives with the principles of the Moral Law over time.

While most Christians grasp this aspect of their faith, they often fail to recognize the crucial link between it and the notion that all civil laws enacted by our governing authorities must align with the Moral Law. Any laws deviating from this alignment are null and void, devoid of any real impact. To put it in perspective, it's akin to passing a law to abolish gravity to prevent frequent falls among the elderly population. Such a law would be null and ineffectual, as gravity operates as an unalterable natural law that cannot be arbitrarily abolished. The same principle applies to laws about morality; God's Moral Law stands as immutable and dependable as gravity itself.*

The initial indicator of whether a governing authority dispenses justice based on biblical principles is its stance on the Moral Law. For instance, consider the recent enactment of the Respect for Marriage Act, which attempted to legalize same-sex marriage. If marriage were a man-made institution, it would be subject to alteration, but it is divinely ordained and remains as unchangeable as gravity. Passing laws that contradict the Moral Law, especially when it becomes a recurring pattern, unequivocally signifies an unjust government.

Another significant criterion for determining whether a governing authority is governing justly is its respect for and safeguarding of fundamental institutions ordained by God in the Bible. These institutions encompass marriage and family, civil government, the church, and the nation of Israel.

Institution of Marriage and Family

The very first human couple, Adam and Eve, established the prototype for marriage. They also formed the initial family unit, laying the foundation for the concept that God's design for

---

* This idea of nullification is important to understand, as it was the operative principle the founders applied in 1776 when they declared independence from England. They listed twenty-seven examples of where the British government had passed laws that violated the Moral Law. More on that in Chapter 3.

marriage involves one man and one woman. This design serves as God's means for the continuation of humanity, with parents bearing the responsibility of having, nurturing, and educating their children in the knowledge of God, enabling them to lead lives that honor Him. This extends to becoming model citizens in their respective communities and nations.

Governments have a role to play in endorsing and supporting God's blueprint for marriage and family through their policies and laws. This involves not only respecting the divine design for the family but also recognizing the binary nature of gender, male and female, as ordained by God (Gen. 1:27, 5:2). Any government that enacts policies and laws undermining the integrity of the family, questioning biological genders, or hindering the educational process for children is, in essence, governing unjustly. Progressive policies in the LGBTQ realm over the past three decades deviate from God's design for marriage and family, serving as a prominent example of unjust governance.

Institution of Civil Government

As previously outlined, we've already discussed the proper role of civil government. Civil leaders who deviate from this role in their positions or impede other branches of government from governing justly can be considered as governing unjustly themselves. A clear example of this occurred in the years leading up to the founding of the United States.

The fundamental principle that the founders applied to their situation was that when a civil authority continuously governs unjustly over an extended period with no intention of changing course, they forfeit their God-given authority to rule. In such cases, Christians should speak out, and resistance becomes appropriate. We have witnessed a similar pattern in America over the past few decades, with the government assuming increasing power over the people and straying far from our constitutional framework. A recent illustration of this was the suspension of religious and civil liberties during the COVID-19 pandemic. Many people were forced to get a new vaccine despite objections to how it was developed (using aborted fetal tissue), and potential adverse health effects (one's body is their most important property). When governing authorities operate outside of the powers granted to them by the consent of the people and restrict fundamental liberties, they are governing unjustly.

Institution of the Church

We are currently in a period known as the Church Age. Jesus entrusted the Church with a commission that includes all races and social classes. During this age, the Church is responsible for making disciples of all nations, which involves various activities, including educating believers about their citizenship role in the civil sphere. Just as with the other institutions ordained by God, *all* civil authorities must respect this role and be open to correction and rebuke from the Church when their actions run counter to the interests of these institutions.

A New Testament example of this is when John the Baptist confronted Herod about marrying his brother's wife (Luke 14:3–4). Similarly, Jesus challenged the Pharisees for failing to uphold justice (Matt. 23:23). Any civil authority that enacts laws and policies restricting the Church from fulfilling its biblical role is governing unjustly.

God's Covenant with Israel

Although Israel is not an institution in the same sense as the others mentioned, God's unconditional covenant with this tiny nation clarifies that He has a unique plan for Israel. God promises to bless this nation, and all other nations are expected to respect His plan. This is why America has traditionally provided unwavering support to Israel. From a pragmatic perspective, history has repeatedly demonstrated that taking an adversarial stance against Israel never ends well for the aggressor nation. Therefore, a governing authority that adopts an anti-Israel stance, particularly when implementing policies detrimental to that nation, is governing contrary to God's will, and therefore governing unjustly.

SUMMARY

In this chapter, we have affirmed the stance of the modern-day evangelical establishment: when civil governments govern justly, our response should be to submit to them and pray for them. We have also provided a clear illustration of what governing justly entails. Civil leaders must respect and uphold these God-ordained institutions to earn the respect and support of the citizenry. In the case of America, this is what the founding generation consented to when they signed the Declaration of Independence. Now, we will turn our attention to how we should respond when civil leaders are governing unjustly.

CHAPTER 4

RESPONSIBILITY OF CHRISTIANS WHEN BEING GOVERNED UNJUSTLY

I n the preceding chapter, we discussed the characteristics of just governance and the appropriate response from citizens when such governance is in place. But what should be the response when a civil authority is governing unjustly? What if the civil authority is not condemning those who do evil but instead is condemning those who are doing what is right? This is the critical question in America today.

The Bible addresses this question for a nation living under a biblical covenant and guides people of faith living under unjust rule. As we read through the Old and New Testaments, we encounter numerous situations where the Israelites were governed unjustly by their kings and when they lived in captivity under unjust foreign civil leaders. Through these accounts, we can observe the various ways in which people of faith responded and how God viewed their actions.

In this chapter, we will explore various biblical responses when civil authority governs unjustly.

RESPONSE WHEN BEING GOVERNED UNJUSTLY

In Romans 13, we are told how civil authorities are to govern, specifically by commending those who do good and bringing punishment to wrongdoers:

> For rulers hold no terror for those who do right, but for those who do wrong. Do you want to be free from fear of the one in authority? Then do what is right and you will be commended. For the one in authority is God's servant for your good. But if you do wrong, be afraid, for rulers do not bear the sword for no reason. They are God's servants, agents of wrath to bring punishment on the wrongdoer. (Rom. 13:3–4)

The question we want to address is: How should Christians react when rulers fail to commend those who do right? What if, even worse, rulers praise wrongdoers and punish those who are doing what is right? Furthermore, how should Christians respond when civil authorities systematically undermine God's institutions, such as marriage and family, civil government, and the church, or become hostile toward the nation of Israel?

When a civil government consistently engages in any of these actions over a prolonged period without any intention of changing course, it is governing unjustly. In such cases, those civil leaders forfeit their God-given role of providing civil leadership, and the people have the God-given right to remove them from office. While we are called to secure justice and should act, individuals choosing to act may suffer unjust consequences, including imprisonment or injury. When citizens find themselves in this situation, they must exercise prudence in their response, considering their specific circumstances and potential negative consequences.

If citizens find themselves living under an unjust civil authority, there are four potential biblical responses:

1. Use every available tool within the legal system to restore justice.
2. Speak out against civil leaders who persistently govern immorally.
3. Engage in civil disobedience when instructed to do something immoral that violates one's conscience.
4. In physical attacks requiring self-defense, individuals or groups may resort to force to oppose or remove an unjust civil authority (the catalyst for the American founding).*

---

* This happened on April 19, 1775, at the battle of Lexington and Concord when the British were planning to seize colonial military supplies. Widely known as the "shot heard around the word," approximately seventy members of the Rev. Clarke's congregation gathered on the lawn of the church to face roughly eight hundred British soldiers. Clarke was committed to the idea that God would only bless a defensive war and instructed his men not to fire unless fired upon. The British did fire first, and eighteen Americans were killed or wounded that day in self-defense (David Barton and Tim Barton, *The American Story*, p. 147-149).

Using the Legal System

The Bible has numerous references to using the justice system to pursue fair judgments both in Israel and under foreign rule. One of the most well-known cases involves two prostitutes who both claimed to be the mother of the same baby (mentioned in Chapter 1). This case likely stood out as the trial of the year, given the challenge of determining the real mother in an era without DNA testing. Solomon proposed a straightforward solution: dividing the baby in half and giving each woman a share. However, the genuine mother passionately pleaded for the child's life and offered to give it to the other woman if it would save her baby. Recognizing the love of the true mother, Solomon delivered the rightful verdict, illustrating the importance of ensuring justice in a case involving individuals from the lowest class of that society (1 Kings 3:16–28).

In Luke 18:1–8, Jesus teaches that God will ensure that justice prevails in the end, even if it is not immediate. He illustrates this point with a parable about a persistent widow who pursued justice through the legal system, where the judge neither feared God nor cared what people thought (verse 2). In the end, the unjust judge granted the widow the justice she sought, even if only out of self-preservation, despite her low standing in her town, which a person like her would have had in that era. Through this example, Jesus emphasizes the importance of perseverance for believers when they are in the right from a civil justice standpoint.

Lastly, in Acts 25:8–12, Paul, a Roman citizen, asserted his rights by appealing to Caesar to hear his case. This was not only proper given his standing as a Roman citizen, but God would use this forum so that many more people would listen to the Gospel as Paul would argue his case.

These examples demonstrate that Christians should not only advocate for equal justice for all but should also be willing to engage in the legal process to defend their causes when necessary. Not only might we be able to correct an injustice, but one also never knows who will be watching and come to know God through our words and actions.

Calling Out Civil Leaders

Unless a civil leader understands the Moral Law is the guiding principle for all forms of jurisprudence, regardless of whether they adhere to Christian beliefs, there is a risk that civil leaders will stray from the moral and ethical conduct expected by God. This is especially relevant for leaders with significant power. That is why it is crucial for citizens, particularly the press, to ask questions and bring attention to actions that violate the Moral Law.

We observe this behavior in both the Old and New Testaments, in Israel and under foreign rule:

- Nathan called out David on his adultery with Bathsheba and having her husband murdered on the battlefield (2 Sam. 12:7–9).
- John the Baptist called out Herod for marrying his brother's wife (Luke 3:19; Matt. 14:1–12).
- Jesus rebuked the Pharisees for neglecting justice:

> Woe to you, teachers of the law and Pharisees, you hypocrites! You give a tenth of your spices—mint, dill and cumin. But you have neglected the more important matters of the law—justice, mercy and faithfulness. You should have practiced the latter, without neglecting the former. (Matt. 23:23)

This does not mean we should spend all our days condemning anyone we see committing grievous sins. Instead, we should address a consistent pattern of injustice and immoral rule, especially when it affects those who cannot defend themselves. Calling out injustices is not unloving; neglecting injustice is unloving.

Civil Disobedience

In biblical terms, civil disobedience occurs when a follower of God refuses to comply with a mandate from civil authorities that is immoral or conflicts with their conscience. The Bible provides many examples of such instances where individuals disobeyed guidance from corrupt leaders:

The Jewish midwives: Pharaoh ordered the midwives to kill the newborn boys just before Moses was born, but they disobeyed this direct order and even lied to him about it (Exod. 1:15–19).

Shadrach, Meshach, and Abednego: These three young Israelites were taken into Babylonian captivity, where King Nebuchadnezzar commanded them to bow down and worship an idol. They refused, and the king had them thrown into a furnace for their disobedience. In this case, God spared their lives (Dan. 3:8–30).

Daniel and the lion's den: Daniel was a trusted adviser to King Darius, but his enemies were determined to frame him. They persuaded King Darius to pass a law prohibiting anyone from praying to anyone other than the king for thirty days. Knowing Daniel's practice of praying three times daily, they reported his disobedience to the King. Consequently, Daniel was thrown into the lion's den for breaking the decree, but God spared him. Darius ended up throwing those who had falsely accused him, along with their families, into the lion's den, where they met their end. (Dan. 6:10–28).

The Apostles: As the early church expanded, the Pharisees ordered the Apostles to stop preaching about Jesus. This directive contradicted what they believed they were commanded to do in their consciences. Despite the orders from the Pharisees, they continued to share the gospel, and God blessed their efforts (Acts 5:27–29).

Civil disobedience has proven to be an effective strategy for addressing injustices, particularly in the latter half of the twentieth century.[*] It is crucial, however, for Christians to exercise prudence and consider the potential consequences of their actions in such cases. Sometimes, God may offer protection to

---

[*] Martin L. King's approach to civil rights in the 1960s was a good example of civil disobedience leading to a positive result.

those opposing immoral rule while other times, He may not. Ultimately, our decisions will depend on prayer and individual conscience, guiding us toward the appropriate course of action based on the specific circumstances.

Self-Defense

The right of self-defense originates from the commandment that protects life, as found in verses such as Genesis 9:5–6 (I will demand an accounting for the life of another human being) and Exodus 20:13 (You shall not murder). If someone else's life is to be protected, then you also have the right to protect your own life.

Let us look at how this applies in the home. During a home invasion, when the lives of a man's wife or child are threatened, it is clear that man is justified in protecting his family as well as his own life. Few would argue against the position that it is his responsibility to protect his family, even to the point of killing the attacker if done in self-defense. If he has this responsibility to his family, why would he not also have a similar responsibility in the community where he lives, enjoying the rights, protection, and the ability to provide for his family that the community provides?

Citizens consenting to live in a community or nation under a covenant are obligated to protect their fellow citizens from being murdered. This obligation extends to protecting your own life if attacked and protecting your neighbor's life.

In today's more civilized society, fewer and fewer people train in the martial arts, so self-defense is abstract to many. However, in the Old Testament, the importance of self-defense was repeatedly reinforced because there were many godless nations, and it was a more necessary skill to have. There are many examples of this, including Abraham rescuing Lot and his family (Gen. 14:11–16), David's confrontation with Goliath (1 Sam. 17), and others:

> Praise be to the LORD my Rock, who trains my hands for war, my fingers for battle. (Ps. 144:1)

> David recognized God gifting him for battle.

> There is a time for everything, and a season for every activity under the heavens ... a time to love and a time to hate, a time for war and a time for peace. (Ecc. 3:1, 8)

> Solomon acknowledged there is a season for peace and war.

> Do not repay anyone evil for evil. Be careful to do what is right in the eyes of everyone. If it is possible, as far as it depends on you, live at peace with everyone. Do not take revenge, my dear friends, but leave room for God's wrath, for it is written: "It is mine to avenge; I will repay," says the Lord. (Rom. 12:17–19)

> Paul urging believers to live in peace *if we are able to.*

Some point to Jesus's teaching in the Sermon on the Mount in Matthew 5 to argue that Christians should never resist an evil person. However, in this passage, the intent is to confront vigilantism (using "eye for an eye" and "tooth for a tooth" for retribution, verse 38) and to present a challenging vision of what love looks like (loving your enemy even when they persecute you or strike you, verses 39–44). This does not mean that God no longer cares about justice or self-defense, as Jesus clearly addresses these issues elsewhere in the New Testament:

> But understand this: if the owner of the house had known at what time of night the thief was coming, he would have kept watch and would not have let his house be broken into. (Matt. 24:43)

> He said to them, "But now if you have a purse, take it, and also a bag; and if you don't have a sword, sell your cloak and buy one." (Luke 22:36)

Finally, when Jesus called out the Pharisees in Matthew 23:23 for neglecting justice (as cited earlier), he reinforced the importance of civil justice for all individuals, initially established in Genesis 9 to protect life. In making this statement about the importance of justice to the Jewish leaders for all individuals, he also affirmed a person's right to defend themselves against an attack on their own life.

The Bible guides our individual relationships with others (to love and forgive) and our civil relationships in communities and nations (to seek liberty and justice for all). When citizens are abused or attacked by their governing authority over an extended period with no intention of change, they are justified in resisting and confronting their civil authority out of self-defense. However, they must apply prudence to their unique situation, weighing their actions based on their conscience and what God may call them to do.

SEVERAL PRACTICAL EXAMPLES

There are several modern examples in North America where citizens sought a more just governing authority. One of these instances happened by accident, while the other arose out of necessity by following the biblical principles for confronting unjust rule and led to the founding of a new nation.

The Plymouth Colony: 1620

The Pilgrims boarded the Mayflower in 1620, seeking religious freedom in the New World. They hoped to find a governing environment that would provide liberty and justice in line with their understanding of biblical principles for civil government. They had the intention of joining the colony at Jamestown; however, they arrived far north of their destination. When prevailing winds prevented them from sailing south, they concluded it was God's will for them to settle where they landed, which is now Plymouth, Massachusetts. However, they encountered an unforeseen problem: they had no official civil government.

Following their faith, they drafted a unique document aboard the Mayflower that became their founding covenant.

The Mayflower Compact, as it is known today, followed the biblical template for starting a community. They followed the same four-step process for creating their community that Israel followed under the leadership of Moses: *acknowledging* God, *appealing* to Him for help, *committing* through the custom of the day, and *declaring* it publicly. You can see this by reading through this incredible document:

> In the name of God, Amen. We, whose names are under-written, the loyal subjects of our dread Sovereign Lord King James, by the Grace of God, of Great Britain, France, and Ireland, King, defender of the Faith, etc.
>
> Having undertaken for the Glory of God, and advance-ment of the Christian faith, and the honor of our King and Country, a voyage to plant the first colony in the Northern parts of Virginia; do by these presents, solemnly and mutu-ally, in the presence of God and one another, covenant and combine ourselves together into a civil body politic; for our better ordering and preservation, and furtherance of the ends aforesaid; and by virtue hereof to enact, consti-tute, and frame, such just and equal laws, ordinances, acts, constitutions, and offices, from time to time, as shall be thought most meet and convenient for the general good of the colony; unto which we promise all due submission and obedience.

In witness whereof we have hereunto subscribed our names at Cape Cod the 11th of November, in the year of the reign of our Sovereign Lord King James, of England, France, and Ireland, the eighteenth, and of Scotland the fifty-fourth, 1620.[14]

ACKNOWLEDGE GOD

Recall acknowledging God in a covenant means calling on God directly and stating the purpose of the covenant. Their covenant starts by acknowledging God with the phrase, "In the name of God." They then clarify what God expects with a civil political body in the body of the text where they,

> solemnly and mutually, in the presence of God and one another, covenant and combine ourselves together into a civil body politic; for our better ordering and preservation, and furtherance of the ends aforesaid; and by virtue hereof to enact, constitute, and frame, such just and equal laws, ordinances, acts, constitutions, and offices, from time to time, as shall be thought most meet and convenient for the general good of the colony.[15]

In just a few words, they summarize their understanding of the theology of civil government. In doing so, they acknowledge what they believe God expects from them as they set out to form a new community.

APPEAL TO GOD

The appeal to God occurs in several ways. First, it happens during the document's drafting when they call on God in the first sentence. Second, they conclude that first sentence with the word "Amen." Christians commonly use this word when ending a prayer, and it means "let it be so." In this case, they start the document with this phrase. It is as if they recognize they are embarking on something very unusual and unprecedented. Even though their pastor, John Robinson, taught that this is what the Bible prescribes, it had never been done before. It is like they were saying, "God, as we embark on starting this community to honor you, *let it be so.*"

In hindsight, it seems evident that they were doing the right thing, but it takes immense courage when you are the first to do something that has never been done before.

COMMIT TO THE COVENANT

This is demonstrated in several ways in their document. First, they explicitly mention it in the text that they,

> do by these presents, solemnly and mutually, in the presence of God and one another, covenant and combine ourselves together into a civil body politic[16]

Second, they signed the document, which was (and still is) today's custom when executing a legal proceeding.

DECLARE IT PUBLICLY

This document was signed on board the Mayflower, making it known to all those present, both passengers staying and the crew heading back to England. They also noted the time and place, rendering it legally binding:

> In witness whereof we have hereunto subscribed our names at Cape Cod the 11th of November, in the year of the reign of our Sovereign Lord King James, of England, France, and Ireland, the eighteenth, and of Scotland the fifty-fourth, 1620.[17]

The drafting and adoption of this first voluntary covenant in the New World was unique, not only because it was the first time this process was followed by the group establishing the civil authority but also because they adhered to the biblical template for starting a community to the letter.

The United States of America: 1776

The American founding happened out of necessity, unlike the events of 1620 with the Pilgrims. What led to the American founding was a British government systematically taking away the rights the colonists had come to enjoy and expect, especially as fellow British citizens. This began after the French and Indian War ended in 1763. Defending the colonies was expensive, so the British government decided to levy taxes on the colonies to replenish the British treasury. From 1764 through 1775, the British passed over a dozen acts designed to raise funds and suppress opposition. These laws were passed without the involvement or consent of the colonies.

The imposition of these laws without the colonists' consent was contrary to what they had become accustomed to, given what they had learned and exercised as their biblical responsibility to govern themselves and given they were largely on their own, living on the edge of the known world. Instead of continuing to grant the colonists the autonomy to govern themselves and pass laws in harmony with the Moral Law, England began asserting more top-down oversight. This resulted in the steady usurpation of the colonists' rights, even though they still considered themselves British citizens.

The colonists were not silent as these events unfolded. They sought redress through various means, but each time, the king put more pressure on the colonies to get them to comply. By June 1776, it became clear to the thirteen colonies that England planned to govern them as a police state, where none of their rights would be secure. The time had come to decide if they should submit to biblically unjust rule or follow in the path of their forefathers and assert what they believed was their God-given right to be governed justly and form a new nation. They did not make this decision quickly or without debate. There were thirteen separate colonies that did not agree on all issues. But they could agree on the biblical basics of governing, which eventually allowed them to unify and separate from England.

They knew they were establishing a new nation. They also recognized the biblical model for this process, particularly the need for a covenant in which they would explain the reasons for their separation and publicly commit to it. A simple reading of their Declaration of Independence reveals that they followed the biblical four-step nation-starting blueprint to the letter.

ACKNOWLEDGE GOD

The colonists acknowledged God and His intention for civil government in the first two paragraphs of the Declaration:

> WHEN in the Course of human events, it becomes necessary for one people to dissolve the political bands which have connected them with another, and to assume among the powers of the earth, the separate and equal station to which the Laws of Nature and of Nature's God entitle them, a decent respect to the opinions of mankind requires that they should declare the causes which impel them to the separation.

> WE hold these truths to be self-evident, that all Men are created equal, that they are endowed by their Creator with certain unalienable Rights, that among these are Life, Liberty and the pursuit of Happiness—That to secure these rights, Governments are instituted among Men, deriving their just powers from the consent of the Governed.[18]

We see several important theological points in these two paragraphs:

1. A timeless Moral Law is known both through conscience and reason and revealed to mankind through the Bible. This comes from the phrase "the Law of Nature and of Nature's God," which Sir William Blackstone explained:

> Man, considered as a creature, must necessarily *be subject to the laws of his creator,* for he is entirely a dependent being. . . . It is necessary that he should in all points conform to his maker's will. *This will of his maker is called the law of nature.* . . . It is binding over all the globe, in all countries, and at all times: no human laws are of any validity, if contrary to this. . . . *The doctrines thus delivered we call the revealed or divine law, and they are to be found only in the holy scriptures.* . . . Upon these two foundations, *the law of nature and the law of revelation,* depend all human laws; that is to say, no human laws should be suffered to contradict these.[19]

2. This law established a timeless standard for nations (the powers of the earth) on how to govern their citizens. Numerous quotes from the founding generation confirm they believed in the ultimate authority of the Moral Law. James Otis was a prominent lawyer in Boston and representative of the Massachusetts General Court. In February of 1761, he argued:

> There must be in every instance, a higher authority, viz. God. Should an act of parliament be against any of his natural laws, which are immutably true, their declaration would be contrary to eternal truth, equity, and justice, and consequently void.[20]

John Jay was New York delegate to the 1st Continental Congress, President of the Congress, Signer of the Treaty of Paris, and First Chief Justice of the Supreme Court. Writing to a friend in 1818 he said:

> Legal punishments are adjusted and inflicted by the law and magistrate, and not by unauthorized individuals. These and all other positive laws or ordinances established by Divine direction, must of necessity be consistent with the moral law.[21]

3. All people are entitled to live by this standard, as it has been given to us by God, and therefore it is a God-given right.
4. Rejecting a governing authority with this God-given responsibility should be explained to all nations (as it may appear to violate Romans 13).
5. Everyone is created equal before God. This means we are equally accountable to God, not that we will all have equal capabilities or material blessings in this life.
6. God is sovereign and grants everyone individual rights that cannot be taken away.

7. We have the right to our lives, religious and civil liberty, and the pursuit of happiness (pursuing God or not, as one's conscience dictates).

8. God instituted civil government which gets its legitimate authority based on the consent of the people. Citizens elect their leaders, expecting these leaders would govern according to these principles.

The founders combined these theological points in several sentences that most Americans still recognize today. In doing so, they provided the rationale to separate from England. They also asserted that confronting an unjust government is what God expects when citizens are being governed unjustly over a long period of time and the civil authority has no intention of changing course.

In the following sections of the Declaration, they explain their unique situation and list twenty-seven examples of how the British government had been systematically violating their unalienable rights. This serves as evidence, submitted to the world, that the British government had been governing immorally and had no intention of changing course.

APPEAL TO GOD

In the last paragraph, after explaining their beliefs on the purpose of civil government and how the British government had been violating their rights, the founders make a formal appeal to God to come to their aid and support their efforts:

We, therefore, the Representatives of the United States of America, in General Congress, Assembled, *appealing to the Supreme Judge of the world for the rectitude of our intentions,* do, in the Name, and by Authority of the good People of these Colonies, solemnly publish and declare, that these United Colonies are, and of Right ought to be Free and Independent States.[22]

As part of their appeal, they also ask God to confirm their motives with the phrase "for the rectitude of our intentions" (rectitude means truthfulness). The founders were not only asking God for help in this dire situation; they were asking God to confirm that they were correct in stating their vision and purpose for civil government and their argument that the British had violated their governing responsibility to such a degree that separation was the only answer.

The word "solemnly" also reinforces the idea that they saw their appeal as a religious action. Given all this, it is clear the founders were making an earnest appeal to God, based on their faith, to help them build a new nation based on this covenant.

COMMIT TO THE COVENANT

The founders' commitment to the Declaration as a formal covenant was evident in several ways. First, in the last sentence, they made a formal pledge expressing their total commitment to see the separation through:

And for the support of this Declaration, with a firm reliance on the protection of divine Providence, *we mutually pledge to each other our Lives, our Fortunes and our sacred Honor.*[23]

With these words, they expressed the full extent of their commitment, including their property and very lives. It's important to note that they emphasized their expectation of God's help to see the separation through, even in the face of the potential loss of everything they held dear. Most of those who signed the Declaration did lose everything, and many did not survive the war. History shows they lived up to their pledge.

Their second act of commitment was signing the document. It is critical to note that signing meant they would be subject to charges of treason if captured. In such a scenario, they would likely have been transported back to England to face trial and execution. Despite this grim prospect, they signed the document, solidifying their total commitment to the cause.

DECLARE IT PUBLICLY

There are several ways in which the founders adhered to the principle of publicly declaring their covenant. First, the document's name, the Declaration of Independence, signifies their commitment to declare it publicly. Second, they published the document and had it read aloud across the colonies. George Washington had the Declaration read to the Continental Army to clarify the reasons for their fight and their ultimate goal—establishing a new nation. Additionally, the founders sent the Declaration to England to ensure that the English understood their reasons for rejecting British rule and their determination, with God's help, to see the action through.

At the time, there was little reason to believe the separation would succeed, but God blessed their actions. Many have tried to attribute America's success to various reasons, but at the core of the separation's success is that the founders followed the biblical template for reacting to long-term unjust rule and establishing a new, God-honoring nation. They *acknowledged* God, *appealed* to Him for help, *committed* to the covenant, and *declared* it to the world.

The American founding was an exception compared to the typical historical pattern, where citizens traded one set of rulers for another through revolution with no mention or application of God's template for governing justly. The founders followed a different path, applying a biblical blueprint to establish a nation that honored God. They used the Moral Law as the foundation for individual and civic life, creating an environment of individual liberty where everyone can go on their own faith journey and choose whether to accept the gospel or not. This environment also allowed individuals to pursue their interests and reach their full potential. When an entire citizenry has this opportunity, the whole nation benefits (becomes *fruitful*), in line with the principles outlined in Genesis 1:28 and 9:1, 7.

Many today view the Declaration as if it were a news bulletin to England, relevant then but considered old news today. However, it is more than that; it is a covenant that makes a set of demanding claims about God's purpose and the objective of civil government. These are claims that assert every citizen must live a certain way.[24] Every American citizen, from the past to the present, must pause to consider these claims and decide whether they will accept and commit to the American founding covenant. This is not a decision to be taken lightly, for everyone who claims to be an American should have an equal level of commitment to defending the covenant and pledging their lives, fortunes, and sacred honor.

Every nation has the same opportunity to follow this biblical blueprint and experience similar blessings from God. This is what He desires and encourages all nations to aspire to, especially Israel. The Bible reveals God's timeless patience, tenderness, and love for Israel, desiring their repentance and a return to their covenant. When Israel or any other nation turns its back on God, however, history demonstrates that they bring ruin upon themselves.

Today, America still stands apart from other nations, but it is in trouble. This "American experiment" in biblically based self-government can continue, but only if we turn our hearts back to God and recommit to our national founding covenant.

SUMMARY

Confronting unjust government can be one of the most challenging aspects of living out one's faith for Christians. However, this is precisely what God calls citizens of all nations to do. We have provided numerous biblical examples across various situations that offer clear guidance on when and how people of faith should act when governed unjustly. America was not only founded under such circumstances, but throughout our nation's history, we have repeatedly risen to the occasion when significant injustices occur at home and abroad.

As we approach our 250th birthday as a nation, America is at a crossroads. Similar to Israel during much of the Old Testament, we are witnessing America's steady decline and struggling to reembrace our founding principles. However, the Bible provides the roadmap back to God's blessing, which becomes evident when we revisit the Old Testament and examine the steps several Old Testament leaders took to regain God's blessings on the nation of Israel. We will explore that in the next chapter.

CHAPTER 5

THE TIMELESS BIBLICAL BLUEPRINT TO RESTORE A WAYWARD NATION

I n the previous chapter, we discussed the characteristics of an unjust government and four potential Christian responses. This chapter will explore the biblical template for restoring a wayward nation to God. As in previous chapters, we will find clear steps and examples in the Bible of nations that turned back to God.

THERE IS NOTHING NEW UNDER THE SUN

Much like the patterns Solomon observes recurring throughout history in the book of Ecclesiastes, the rise and fall of nations follow a similar pattern. This should give us comfort and hope that while God will judge wayward nations, there is a biblical blueprint for restoring a nation that turns away from God. This cycle of repentance and renewal can be seen in the history of Israel, starting with Moses:

> Moses summoned all the Israelites and said to them: "Your eyes have seen all that the LORD did in Egypt to Pharaoh, to all his officials and to all his land. With your own eyes you saw those great trials, those signs and great wonders. But to this day the LORD has not given you a mind that understands or eyes that see or ears that hear. Yet the LORD says, 'During the forty years that I led you through the wilderness, your clothes did not wear out, nor did the sandals on your feet. You ate no bread and drank no wine or other fermented drink. I did this so that you might know that I am the LORD your God.'
>
> When you reached this place, Sihon king of Heshbon and Og king of Bashan came out to fight against us, but we defeated them. We took their land and gave it as an inheritance to the Reubenites, the Gadites and the half-tribe of Manasseh.
>
> Carefully follow the terms of this covenant, so that you may prosper in everything you do. All of you are standing today in the presence of the LORD your God—your leaders and chief men, your elders and officials, and all the other men of Israel, together with your children and your wives, and the foreigners living in your camps who chop your wood and carry your water. You are standing here in

order to enter into a covenant with the LORD your God, a covenant the LORD is making with you this day and sealing with an oath, to confirm you this day as his people, that he may be your God as he promised you and as he swore to your fathers, Abraham, Isaac and Jacob. I am making this covenant, with its oath, not only with you who are standing here with us today in the presence of the LORD our God but also with those who are not here today." (Deut. 29:2–15)

This occurs near the end of Moses's life when he reminds them of their covenant made decades earlier. They are not expected to keep the law perfectly, but they are expected to govern justly, acknowledging God and His Moral Law as the legal standard. Even with this reminder, he tells them they will be judged in the future and explains why:

And the answer will be: "It is *because this people abandoned the covenant of the LORD*, the God of their ancestors, the covenant he made with them when he brought them out of Egypt. They went off and worshiped other gods and bowed down to them, gods they did not know, gods he had not given them. Therefore the LORD's anger burned against this land, so that he brought on it all the curses written in this book." (Deut. 29:25–27)

Again, this is not a condemnation for failing to keep the Moral Law perfectly; it is for chronically disregarding their national founding covenant first established in Exodus 19–24.

They were neither acknowledging God and His Moral Law nor governing justly.

WHAT IS REQUIRED TO HAVE GOD INTERVENE

The Bible provides a very clear and straightforward path for nations to be restored to God, with advice that He gave to Solomon:

> When I shut up the heavens so that there is no rain, or command locusts to devour the land or send a plague among my people, if my people, who are called by my name, *will humble themselves and pray and seek my face and turn from their wicked ways, then I will hear from heaven, and I will forgive their sin and will heal their land.* (2 Chron. 7:13–14)

The simple answer is that if a wayward nation realizes its offense towards God and wishes to seek restoration, it must humble itself and turn from its wicked ways. This *must be done corporately*, however, versus through individual prayers. As with Israel, this essentially involves following the same four-step process they used when they were originally established: acknowledging their sins as transgressions against God's Moral Law, appealing to God for help by seeking His face, recommitting to their covenant by offering sacrifices (according to the custom of the day), and declaring their intent to recommit to God to the world.

The most extravagant example of recommitting to Israel's national covenant was when Solomon ascended to power. King David was ruling, and things in Israel were generally good, although the transition after David died was rocky for a time. Solomon came to power and began construction of the temple. When it was completed, a dedication service was held where he acknowledged the original covenant made through Moses and promised to govern justly (1 Kings 8:1–66):

> The LORD has kept the promise he made: I have succeeded David my father and now I sit on the throne of Israel, just as the LORD promised, and I have built the temple for the Name of the LORD, the God of Israel. I have provided a place there for the ark, in which is the covenant of the LORD that he made with our ancestors when he brought them out of Egypt. (1 Kings 8:20–21)

> LORD, the God of Israel, there is no God like you in heaven above or on earth below—you who keep your covenant of love with your servants who continue wholeheartedly in your way. (1 Kings 8:23)

> Praise be to the LORD, who has given rest to his people Israel just as he promised. Not one word has failed of all the good promises he gave through his servant Moses. May the LORD our God be with us as he was with our ancestors; may he never leave us nor forsake us. May he turn our hearts to him, to walk in obedience to him and

keep the commands, decrees and laws he gave our ancestors. And may these words of mine, which I have prayed before the LORD, be near to the LORD our God day and night, that he may uphold the cause of his servant and the cause of his people Israel according to each day's need, so that all the peoples of the earth may know that the LORD is God and that there is no other. And may your hearts be fully committed to the LORD our God, to live by his decrees and obey his commands, as at this time. (1 Kings 8: 56–61)

Following the custom of the day, they offered more sacrifices than could be counted (verse 5). They celebrated for 14 days (verse 65). This was perhaps the greatest national recommitment in world history. God blessed Israel, until Solomon began to be influenced by his many wives and started to worship foreign gods. As wise as he was, he was not immune to turning away from God. After he died, the nation was divided and began another downward cycle.

After Solomon's reign, we observe that many Old Testament Kings turned away from God and were judged. Nonetheless, several commendable civil leaders, such as Josiah and Nehemiah, heeded the advice from Moses and Solomon. At the commencement of their reign, they renewed their national covenant with their fellow citizens, and God blessed their rule—for a season.

Josiah became king at the age of thirteen, roughly three centuries after Solomon. Early in his reign, he decided to restore the temple, and during the renovation process, the Book of Moses was discovered. After the book was read to the young king, he recommitted to Israel's national covenant in the pattern of Moses and Solomon. God blessed his reign—for a season:

> Then the king called together all the elders of Judah and Jerusalem. He went up to the temple of the LORD with the people of Judah, the inhabitants of Jerusalem, the priests and the prophets—all the people from the least to the greatest. He read in their hearing all the words of the Book of the Covenant, which had been found in the temple of the LORD. The king stood by the pillar and renewed the covenant in the presence of the LORD—to follow the LORD and keep his commands, statutes and decrees with all his heart and all his soul, thus confirming the words of the covenant written in this book. Then all the people pledged themselves to the covenant. (2 Kings 23:1–3)

Nehemiah returned to Israel in 444 BC and rebuilt the wall around Jerusalem. When complete, he followed the same practice and had Ezra read the Book of the Law to the people. Afterward, they also recommitted to their national covenant. As in the past, God blessed their community—for a season:

> They stood where they were and read from the Book of the Law of the LORD their God for a quarter of the day, and spent another quarter in confession and in worshiping the LORD their God. . . . In view of all this, we are making a binding agreement, putting it in writing, and our leaders,

our Levites and our priests are affixing their seals to it. (Neh. 9:3, 38)

The actions of these later two civil leaders are also consistent with instruction from Job 36:

If they obey and serve him, they will spend the rest of their days in prosperity and their years in contentment. But if they do not listen, they will perish by the sword and die without knowledge. (Job 36:11–12)

While we tend to focus on how God judged Israel in the Old Testament, we also find several examples of civil leaders in Gentile nations who repented, and God healed their land. The first is Jonah calling on Nineveh to repent:

The word of the LORD came to Jonah son of Amittai: "Go to the great city of Nineveh and preach against it, because its wickedness has come up before me." (Jonah 1:1–2)

Jonah obeyed the word of the LORD and went to Nineveh. Now Nineveh was a very large city; it took three days to go through it. Jonah began by going a day's journey into the city, proclaiming, "Forty more days and Nineveh will be overthrown." The Ninevites believed God. A fast was proclaimed, and all of them, from the greatest to the least, put on sackcloth. When Jonah's warning reached the king of Nineveh, he rose from his throne, took off his royal robes, covered himself with sackcloth and sat down in the dust. This is the proclamation he issued in Nineveh: "By the decree of the king and his nobles: Do not let people or animals, herds or flocks, taste anything; do not let them eat or drink. But let people and animals be covered with sackcloth. Let everyone call urgently on God. Let them give up their evil ways and their violence. Who knows? God may yet relent and with compassion turn from his fierce anger so that we will not perish." When God saw what they did and how they turned from their evil ways, he relented and did not bring on them the destruction he had threatened. (Jonah 3:3–10)

The second example is of Nebuchadnezzar when ruling Babylon. God warned him in a dream that Daniel interpreted for him, explaining the King would lose his kingdom for seven years until he acknowledged God and he repented. Notice, however, that Daniel encourages him to renounce his sins so that maybe his prosperity might continue:

This is the interpretation, Your Majesty, and this is the decree the Most High has issued against my LORD the king: You will be driven away from people and will live with the wild animals; you will eat grass like the ox and be drenched with the dew of heaven. Seven times will pass by for you until you acknowledge that the Most High is sovereign over all kingdoms on earth and gives them to anyone he wishes. The command to leave the stump of the tree with its roots means that your kingdom will be restored to you when you acknowledge that Heaven rules. Therefore, Your Majesty, be pleased to accept my advice: Renounce your sins by doing what is right, and your wickedness by being kind to the oppressed. It may be that then your prosperity will continue.

All this happened to King Nebuchadnezzar. Twelve months later, as the king was walking on the roof of the royal palace of Babylon, he said, "Is not this the great Babylon I have built as the royal residence, by my mighty power and for the glory of my majesty?" Even as the words were on his lips, a voice came from heaven, "This is what is decreed for you, King Nebuchadnezzar: Your royal authority has been taken from you. You will be driven away from people and will live with the wild animals; you will eat grass like the ox. Seven times will pass by for you until you acknowledge that the Most High is sovereign over all kingdoms on earth and gives them to anyone he wishes." (Dan. 4:24–32)

All of this happened, and after seven years, his sanity was restored. Afterward, he praised God, and his kingdom was restored. The pattern is the same: when any community or nation honors God, He tends to bless them, but when they turn away from Him, they face judgment, the very cycle of blessing and judgment that Moses explained to the Israelites.

THIS CAN WORK TODAY

Today's big question for many American patriots is: How can we turn America around? How can we hope to restore the principles of liberty and justice for all when our culture is so divided? The answer is: follow the same template as the Jewish and Gentile civil leaders did in the Bible. But how might this look in twenty-first-century America? Are things not far worse today than during the founding era?

The situation today is very similar to the founding era. During the World Wars, the enemy was on foreign lands, and during the Civil War, there was a clear dividing line between the northern and southern states. Today, patriots and Progressives live side by side across our nation, much like in the 1770s. Instead of Progressives, some Loyalists collaborated with the all-powerful British government to turn in those fighting against the crown. Today, many Progressive citizens working with fellow Progressives in positions of power are unjustly persecuting American patriots.

If God could come to the aid of the founding generation, surely He can come to the aid of faithful Patriots today. Just as the founders followed the four-step process of acknowledging God, appealing to Him for help, committing their lives, fortunes, and sacred honor, and declaring their intentions to seek to govern justly, we must do the same.

How might this work in America today? What series of events might have to happen for God to forgive and restore our nation? Conditions are different today than during the founding era, but if we were to apply the biblical template the founders followed, it might look something like this:

- Have a national gathering of like-minded, nationally recognized spiritual and civil leaders consider the question, "Do we still hold to the American founding covenant, including the Law of Nature and Nature's God—that is, the Moral Law—as God's standard?" This group might include current and former government officials who believe in our founding national covenant. It should also include nationally recognized Judeo-Christian spiritual leaders. They do not need to agree on many doctrinal positions other than the Moral Law and the basic principles of governing presented in earlier chapters.

- Document a list of immoral offenses pushed by Progressive ideology that constitute how America has dishonored God in recent decades. This list would be an updated version of a long train of abuses the founders listed in 1776.

- Draft a statement affirming the Declaration and our collective commitment to restoring America to a God-honoring nation by upholding the Moral Law as the rule of law.

- Recommit to our national founding covenant with a formal signing ceremony, covered in prayer. The recommitment document could be published online for any American to affix their signature to, signifying the people's commitment.

- This should be followed by periodic and ongoing prayer and fasting by all those Americans, showing commitment and reliance on God to do what is impossible for us to do on our own.

This plan may seem naive, but do we truly believe we can reverse America's decline without God's help? Are we counting on our politicians to somehow craft new policies, expressed in just the right way, such that we might turn the tide?

If we agree that we need God's help, why would we not follow the biblical template so clearly explained through multiple Old Testament situations? The founders did, and we are a nation today because of their devotion to God's plan for government. The Bible is clear: garnering God's support requires a national intervention by the people, led by spiritual and civil leaders. This is where we acknowledge our national sins and plead for His help to heal our land and restore us to a God-honoring nation.

As the founding demonstrated, it does not have to be supported by the entire country; still, it must be an active, concerted effort by a dedicated critical mass sincerely seeking God's help. I believe that such a critical mass exists in America today.[*] We need to be pointed in the right direction to recommit to our national founding covenant: the Declaration of Independence.

---

[*] Estimates are that between 30 percent and 50 percent of the colonials favored independence in the 1770s, mostly likely a clear minority. I believe there are at least this many Americans today, if not many more, who wish to see America restored to our founding principles.

MOTIVATION

Several factors should inspire Christians to take action when governed unjustly. First and foremost, we have argued that it is our citizenship duty to do so. How individuals act may vary based on their unique gifts and abilities, and this diversity makes the church beautiful. Some may be capable of directly challenging illegitimate or brazen, covenant-breaking civil leaders. Others may be gifted in providing support through financial aid, political engagement, or prayer. When people of faith find themselves in this situation, they must leverage all the gifts among the citizenry to confront injustice and restore civil order. This is how we live out our faith in this area, and the church is responsible for conveying this to anyone willing to hear.

Another motivating factor for Christians to take action is the understanding that God will judge nations that openly defy Him, especially when there is little to no resistance to the widespread injustice inflicted by a civil government upon its citizens. This is a point upon which God repeatedly challenged Israel:

> The vineyard of the LORD Almighty is the nation of Israel, and the people of Judah are the vines he delighted in. And he looked for justice, but saw bloodshed; for righteousness, but heard cries of distress. (Isa. 5:7)

> This is what the LORD says to you, house of David: "Administer justice every morning; rescue from the hand of the

oppressor the one who has been robbed, or my wrath will break out and burn like fire because of the evil you have done— burn with no one to quench it." (Jer. 21:12)

They trample on the heads of the poor as on the dust of the ground and deny justice to the oppressed. (Amos 2:7)

This is what the LORD Almighty said: "Administer true justice; show mercy and compassion to one another." (Zech. 7:9)

One of the most striking passages that speaks to this point is Jeremiah 6, where God is once again pleading with the Israelites to change course:

This is what the LORD says: "Stand at the crossroads and look; ask for the ancient paths, ask where the good way is, and walk in it, and you will find rest for your souls. But you said, 'We will not walk in it.' I appointed watchmen over you and said, 'Listen to the sound of the trumpet!' But you said, 'We will not listen.'" (Jer. 6:16–17)

God is again pleading with Israel to return to its national covenant, established in Exodus 19–24 through Moses. Then, in a scene reminiscent of an episode of *The Office*, as God's impending judgment looms over His chosen people, Jeremiah figuratively *turns to the camera* and delivers a sobering warning to the nations of the world:

Therefore hear, you nations; you who are witnesses, observe what will happen to them. Hear, you earth: I am bringing disaster on this people, the fruit of their schemes, because they have not listened to my words and have rejected my law. (Jer. 6:18–19)

Later, God confirms His judgment on Israel is due to them not keeping their national covenant established through Moses:

The LORD said to me, "Proclaim all these words in the towns of Judah and in the streets of Jerusalem: *Listen to the terms of this covenant and follow them.* From the time I brought your ancestors up from Egypt until today, I warned them again and again, saying, *Obey me.* But they did not listen or pay attention; instead, they followed the stubbornness of their evil hearts. So *I brought on them all the curses of the covenant I had commanded them to follow but that they did not keep.*" (Jer. 11:6–8)

The judgment upon the Israelites was not because they failed to keep the Moral Law perfectly. It was judgment because they rejected their national founding covenant made through Moses—which God clearly presented as a condition of agreeing to the covenant. While achieving perfect adherence to the Moral Law is impossible, striving to govern according to the principles of self-government in the Bible is entirely feasible. It may be challenging, but governing justly is as attainable as having a successful marriage, raising godly children, or managing one's finances effectively. To suggest otherwise is to question the truth of God's word, as the Bible presents numerous examples of people who lived productive, God-honoring lives—including the establishment and maintenance of civil justice.

Other historical examples of God judging immoral nations include Sodom and Gomorrah, the Canaanites, and the Babylonians. Modern history confirms this same pattern of judgment with the Axis powers of WWII as an example. Germany, Italy, and Japan were utterly defeated because of their unjust rule. History is filled with nations that governed unjustly, and God judged them all. This should motivate all Christians to seek to restore justice in their communities and nations, or they may face similar judgment.

SUMMARY

With American culture descending further and further into chaos, God's people must have the knowledge and conviction to stand up and offer a clear, concise explanation of the root cause of our current state. In doing so, we provide a thoughtful, rational explanation while also sharing our faith, effectively evangelizing in the process.

Furthermore, we are the ones God calls upon to provide the leadership to receive His forgiveness and blessing. It involves confessing our national sins, just as the founding generation did with the British government, and recommitting to the same covenant our founders did. We will undoubtedly face challenges, as that generation did. We may lose everything in the process just as many from the founding generation and many generations since lost everything. Still, in doing so, we honor not only all previous generations who fought to preserve American liberty and justice, we also honor God by living out our faith in this crucial area.

The duty is ours; the results are God's.[25]

CONCLUSION

The churches conflict regarding Christians' proper role in politics persists today. America's decline is due in large part to many churches being unengaged or indifferent to politics. To restore America to its founding principles, this must change.

How is it that committed Christians can be so diametrically opposed on this issue? One side correctly believes that evangelism and discipleship were critical activities that Jesus focused on throughout his earthly ministry. The other side agrees with this idea but *also* believes that Jesus supported the Old Testament, in which God ordained civil government and demanded justice based on the Ten Commandments as the foundation of God's blueprint for just civil authority. How can the first group not see this universal call for justice, which is also clearly taught in the Bible?

A few years ago, I was part of the first group. Growing up, I was taught that America was a Christian nation, although the meaning of that term remained unclear to me. Then, in the 1980s, I began hearing a different narrative, claiming that the founders were deists, and that America was not a noble nation because of their failure to submit to civil leaders over taxation and other issues. The topic of slavery also emerged, along with the assertion that the founders considered slaves as only three-fifths of a person. I heard no compelling biblical arguments to refute these claims, and over time, I embraced this new narrative.

In the 1990s, I started reading books about the founding of America. Around 2000, I turned to the Bible to explore counter-arguments to what I had accepted. To my amazement, I found thousands of verses related to civil government, and after several years, I recognized some justifications for the founding.

Even after encountering these arguments, I still found it difficult to accept the idea that the Revolutionary War could be biblically justifiable. It took several more years, during which I wanted to change my perspective but struggled. I cannot identify the exact moment, but at some point, I suddenly realized that not only was the Revolution biblically justifiable, but also that our Declaration of Independence was, in fact, our national founding covenant. I recognized that our founders followed the biblical template precisely, making America an exceptional nation because they followed that template to the letter. Furthermore, I realized the depth of my responsibility as a Christian living in America under this covenant. I saw that I have a duty, as part of living out my faith, to do everything I could to uphold the pledge I inherited that the founders made in the Declaration.

Having gone through my own journey, I realize how challenging this is for Christians still wrestling with this question. This situation reminds me of optical illusions that initially present a clear image until someone points out a second image. In the figure below, most people will initially see an old woman looking down.[*][26]

Upon closer examination, another image becomes apparent: a younger woman looking back over her right shoulder. Both images are accurate; it's a matter of perspective. Most of us see only one image until someone provides the information that broadens our perspective. And, once you see this additional perspective, it's impossible to unsee it.

This book is dedicated to helping earnest Christians in today's church see the perspective that some of us understand and are committed to living out as an integral part of our faith. As one examines these principles, one will discover an entirely new and exciting dimension of the Christian faith previously hidden from view. One will likely view American history through a different lens, recognizing at a new level the incredible faith and sacrifices made by many of our fellow countrymen to defend the

---

[*] The oldest known image of this type is believed to be from an anonymous German postcard from 1888.

Constitution and our national founding covenant: the Declaration of Independence.

We are living in historic times in the unfolding of the American story. As in the 1770s, the principles and policies being implemented by Progressives are fundamentally contrary to "the Laws of Nature and of Nature's God" that the Declaration of Independence says we are entitled to live by.* Similarly, these Progressive policies have been pushed for decades, leading to a modern-day "long Train of Abuses," also with the aim of imposing a top-down government which will reduce Americans to "absolute Despotism." Just as the founding generation concluded, this current government is governing contrary to biblical principles for a just civil authority captured in the Declaration of Independence and summarized in this book. Per these founding principles, when the government operates this way over a long period with no intent to change, they become illegitimate and should be removed using all legal means. The Declaration tells us our actions require "prudence," with an appeal to "the Supreme Judge of the World for the Rectitude of our Intentions." For this we must recommit to these principles in our founding covenant, the Declaration of Independence, and seek God's favor to restore America to our founding principles.

With a comprehensive biblical understanding of our citizenship duty to help reestablish liberty and justice for all, I believe we stand on the brink of the most significant evangelistic movement in world history. This is because one cannot help but

---

* From the Declaration of Independence, referencing the Moral Law summarized by the Ten Commandments.

share the gospel message when explaining our true American heritage. The church, however, is not prepared to explain the biblical principles behind the American founding or to help lead to a peaceful resolution for the coming struggle.

I hope the truths presented in this book will help Christians see the broader biblical guidance on civil government and recognize that God calls His followers to step forward and lead in this area. Understanding these truths will enable us to explain God's provision for liberty and justice at a time when people will be looking for thoughtful, reasoned answers. These discussions will also create an opportunity to share the gospel in a new way.

To restore America to a God-honoring nation, we must recommit to our national covenant: the Declaration of Independence. Following this biblical template for national reconciliation, we not only invite God to heal our land but also live out an essential part of our faith.

The duty is ours; the results are God's.[27]

Mark Burrell

APPENDIX I

TYPICAL OBJECTIONS

One of the biggest obstacles to Christians reengaging in politics is the objections raised by church leaders, Progressives, and others. In this section, I will briefly address the most common objections given to justify not engaging in politics. A more detailed explanation of many of these objections can be found in my first book, *Rediscovering the American Covenant: Roadmap to Restore America*.

INVOLVEMENT IN POLITICS HAMPERS EVANGELISM

To address this objection, we must first look at the Old Testament and ask, "What was God's evangelistic strategy before Jesus came?" The answer is found in Deuteronomy 4, where Moses communicated that if Israel governed justly, the nations of the world would notice and come to investigate. By doing so,

Israel would serve as a light to the surrounding Gentile nations, and they would observe their culture and learn about God in the process. In 1 Kings 10:1–9, we can see this strategy working perfectly in the account of the visit of the Queen of Sheba. Interestingly, Jesus affirms her conversion in Matthew 12:39–42 when confronting the Pharisees.

The Great Commission by Jesus in Matthew 28 represented a key change in strategy:

> Therefore go and make disciples of all nations, baptizing them in the name of the Father and of the Son and of the Holy Spirit, and teaching them to obey everything I have commanded you. And surely I am with you always, to the very end of the age. (Matt. 28:19–20)

God needed to clarify this new evangelistic approach because He sent His Son to die on the cross for the sins of mankind without asserting His role as the reigning King on earth, which will occur at His second coming. Since Jesus was not establishing His kingdom during His earthly ministry but ushering in a new period in which God would reach out to Gentiles directly with the gospel message, He directed His disciples to GO and spread the gospel to the ends of the earth. Nevertheless, there is more to the question of what Jesus expects from His followers.

Jesus affirmed that everything in the Old Testament was true and should be followed. He never once suggested that civil government, ordained in Genesis 9:5–6, was no longer

important. Paul's reference to God's purpose for civil government in Romans 13 confirmed the principles for a just civil
authority outlined in Genesis 9, to commend those *who do good
and punish wrongdoers*. Romans 13 does not introduce some new
teaching that we submit to civil government no matter what, as
many modern-day pastors teach; it affirms everything taught in
the Old Testament.

Paul also provided guidance on the gifts critical for establishing a just civil authority, including administration, wisdom,
and leadership (Rom. 12; 1 Cor. 12; Eph. 4). Therefore, we
should seek people with these gifts to serve as public leaders.

Lastly, Paul states in 1 Timothy 2 that we should pray for our
civil leaders so that we,

> *may live peaceful and quiet lives in all godliness and holiness.*
> This is good, and pleases God our Savior, who wants all
> people to be saved and to come to a knowledge of the
> truth. (1 Tim. 2:2–4)

In summary, the Great Commission brought a change in
evangelistic strategy and is to be pursued *along with* establishing liberty and justice for all. They are not at odds; in fact, civil
government is God's provision to all of human civilization to
provide law and order. Done correctly, a just civil authority is a
great blessing to the citizenry of all nations who choose to apply
these biblical principles. Doing so enables evangelism and the
pursuit of holy living as one's conscience dictates.

SEPARATION OF CHURCH AND STATE

The phrase "separation of church and state" is frequently employed by both Progressives and Christians to question the role of the Christian faith in the founding and ongoing maintenance of civil governments across America. This phrase was invoked in the 1947 SCOTUS ruling in the case of Everson v. Board of Education.* This case attempted to establish a new legal principle, stating that biblical principles taught by the church should not influence state-sponsored civil authority:

> In the words of Jefferson, the clause against establishment of religion by law was intended to erect "a wall of separation between church and State." . . . That wall must be kept high and impregnable. We could not approve the slightest breach.[28]

Many people assume the phrase "a wall of separation between church and state" is in the Constitution, implying that Christians must not seek to incorporate their faith in the public square. However, it is not found in any founding documents or amendments to the Constitution. The phrase comes from a letter written by Thomas Jefferson in 1802 to the Danbury Baptist Church, whose members had expressed concern that the new government could infringe on the church's right to free speech.

---

* SCOTUS stands for the Supreme Court of the United States.

The established church in Connecticut was the Congregational Church. This group of Baptists hoped that Jefferson's sentiments, which had aided in disestablishing the Anglican Church in Virginia, might also assist in disestablishing the Congregational Church in Connecticut. Ideally, this would influence all other states that still had an established state church that imposed certain religious beliefs on its citizens, removing the threat of imprisonment that many Baptist ministers faced when preaching in states with state-sponsored Christian denominations, such as the Anglican Church in Virginia.

Jefferson's reply was to assure them that the new federal government could not pass a law outlawing the Baptist denomination, thanks to protections provided by the establishment clause in the First Amendment:

> I contemplate with sovereign reverence that act of the whole American people which declared that their legislature should "make no law respecting an establishment of religion, or prohibiting the free exercise thereof," thus building a wall of separation between Church & State.[29]

Jefferson reinforced this view in a letter to Samuel Miller on January 23, 1808:

> I consider the government of the US as interdicted by the constitution from intermeddling with religious institutions, their doctrines, discipline, or exercises. This results not only from the provision that no law shall be made

respecting the establishment, or free exercise, of religion, but from that also which reserves to the states the powers not delegated to the US. Certainly no power to prescribe any religious exercise, or to assume authority in religious discipline, has been delegated to the general [federal] government. . . . Every religious society has a right to determine for itself the times for these exercises, & the objects proper for them, according to their own particular tenets.[30]

Jefferson's stance was the exact opposite of the 1947 ruling attempting to redefine "separation of church and state." Consider the 1799 opinion of Supreme Court Associate Justice Samuel Chase, who also signed the Declaration of Independence, in Runkel v. Winemiller, where he declared the following:

Religion is of general and public concern, and on its support depend, in great measure, the peace and good order of government, the safety and happiness of the people. By our form of government, the Christian religion is the established religion, and all sects and denominations of Christians are placed upon the same equal footing and are equally entitled to protection in their religious liberty.[31]

Like the Dred Scott ruling in 1857 that declared slaves were not protected by the Constitution, the 1947 ruling was clearly incorrect. It contradicted the biblical governing principles in our founding documents and legal precedent during the 150 years after our founding.

THE BIBLE TEACHES THAT WE SHOULD SUBMIT TO CIVIL AUTHORITY

This was answered in earlier chapters, but it is important to address here briefly. Some summary points:

- When examining all of Scripture regarding the purpose and role of civil government, we find instructions on what a just governing authority should resemble.
- When a civil authority is governing justly, Christians are to submit as the Bible prescribes, not only to receive commendation from that governing authority but also to set an example for other nonbelieving citizens.
- When a civil authority is persistently governing unjustly with no intention of changing, Christians should speak up and employ all legal means to restore biblical principles of liberty and justice for all.
- The guiding principle in the American founding was that the British government had been governing unjustly for an extended period with no indication of changing.
- In response to this, the founders followed the biblical template for establishing a God-honoring nation in the Declaration of Independence, which is our national founding covenant.
- By adhering to this template, God has blessed America incredibly while the general citizenry and our civil leaders lived and governed according to our national covenant.

- Today, our governing authority bears a lot of resemblance to the tyranny the colonies were experiencing in the 1770s. Given this, the biblical response is that we should recommit to our national founding covenant, asking God for help to "heal our land" (2 Chron. 7:14) so that we can restore justice.

CHRISTIANS ARE TO LOVE THEIR ENEMIES VERSUS CONFRONT THEM WITH THEIR SIN

One of the most difficult aspects of the Christian faith is loving those who hate God and persecute believers while also not hesitating to call out blatant sinful behavior that can harm individuals, families, and communities. Both are clearly taught in the Bible:

> You have heard that it was said, "Love your neighbor and hate your enemy." But I tell you, love your enemies and pray for those who persecute you, that you may be children of your Father in heaven. (Matt. 5:43–45)

> It is actually reported that there is sexual immorality among you, and of a kind that even pagans do not tolerate: A man is sleeping with his father's wife. And you are proud! Shouldn't you rather have gone into mourning and have put out of your fellowship the man who has been doing this? For my part, even though I am not

physically present, I am with you in spirit. As one who is present with you in this way, I have already passed judgment in the name of our Lord Jesus on the one who has been doing this. So when you are assembled and I am with you in spirit, and the power of our Lord Jesus is present, hand this man over to Satan for the destruction of the flesh, so that his spirit may be saved on the day of the Lord. (1 Cor. 5:1–5)

Churches are covenant communities centered around a set of beliefs summarized by a series of doctrinal statements. The previous example was within a church community, where it is even more important to confront and remove blatant sin. Civil communities that establish themselves based on the biblical template for starting a community are similar. However, they are populated with both believers and unbelievers, which means there will be citizens who willfully, or out of ignorance, disobey God's Moral Law.

The goal is not to go around pointing out everyone's sinful conduct, as we would naturally expect sinful behavior from unbelievers. Instead, it is to confront blatant immoral behavior that undermines the ability to protect the God-given rights of the majority of citizens. Failing to confront evil behavior that infringes on the rights of our fellow citizens is what is actually unloving. Seeking to protect these rights, even giving one's life to secure them, is the ultimate act of love for everyone in a community.

This is the argument we must learn to make.

WHY BOTHER TRYING TO RESTORE LIBERTY AND JUSTICE FOR ALL SINCE WE ARE LIVING IN THE END TIMES?

This line of reasoning is based on two incorrect assumptions that, in the end, offer excuses for doing nothing. The first erroneous assumption is that we can know for sure we are living in the end times simply because the world is, once again, going through a difficult time. Many past generations have believed they were living in the end times because of extraordinary events, yet the world continues on. The Bible is clear, however, that no one knows the hour of the Lord's return (Matt. 24).

This leads to the second flawed assumption: because the Rapture may occur any day, it means we should no longer be obedient to what the Bible calls us to do in certain areas, like civil government. Nowhere does the Bible state that we should be obedient only to select responsibilities during the end times while forsaking others, such as seeking to maintain liberty and justice for all. In this present age, we have various responsibilities that pertain to our personal lives, families, and communities. Until the Lord actually returns or we pass away, we are to persevere in all these areas as part of living out our faith.

CULTURAL AND NATIONAL DECLINE ARE INEVITABLE; THEREFORE, IT IS NOT POSSIBLE TO TURN THINGS AROUND, AND WE SHOULD NOT BOTHER TRYING

The Bible is God's handbook for life. In it, we learn how to conduct ourselves in a way that leads to a productive, fulfilling, and God-honoring life. When the Bible provides guidance on having a successful marriage, raising godly children, or achieving financial security, there is a consensus that by following this guidance, we can generally expect success in these areas, although it is not guaranteed.

The biggest challenge over the course of human history has been living in peace with our neighbors. Whether it is maintaining peaceful relations within or between nations, the Bible is equally informative. As discussed in the earlier chapters of this book, there are thousands of verses where God provides guidance on how nations can secure peace and prosperity if only this guidance were followed. To dismiss all the biblical counsel in this area and declare it hopeless is to accuse God of asking us to do something impossible. But God not only explains the process for nations to be blessed, He also provides several examples in the Old Testament of nations that experienced God's blessing or a reprieve from judgment because they repented (such as Solomon, Josiah, Nehemiah, Nineveh, and Babylon under Nebuchadnezzar).

God clearly calls us to live a certain way as individuals, families, and nations. We see examples in the Bible and in our own lives: it is possible to follow His guidance and be blessed. It may be very difficult, but it is possible.

I CANNOT VOTE FOR A CANDIDATE BECAUSE OF THEIR BACKGROUND OR PERSONALITY

Individual personalities or things they have previously done are certainly a consideration, but there is another question we must ask first. That is, "What does God expect from believers with respect to civil government?"

The objective of this book is to make a clear biblical argument that God expects His followers to step forward and lead in the civil arena to establish liberty and justice for all; in fact, He demands it! Opting out of this responsibility is not an option for believers, yet most evangelical churches treat it as optional. This is why most churches end up ignoring the topic and asking their members not to bring it up.

If one finds the candidates unsatisfactory, the question to ask is, "Who is responsible for identifying and training civil leaders to follow biblical principles?" The answer is clear: Christians, especially church leaders, bear the responsibility for developing and supporting the next generation of civil leaders. Unfortunately, they are often ill-equipped and disinclined to take on this responsibility.

The vast majority of church leaders have not only abdicated their responsibility to identify, train, and encourage the next generation of civil leaders, but they also frequently disparage civic engagement. Most pastors have never delivered a single message on God's expectations regarding civil government; instead, they emphasize evangelism and "building the kingdom" as more spiritually significant activities. This alienates those who feel called to engage or serve, especially in the military. While many churches still display the flag on Memorial Day to thank veterans for their service, by downplaying civil service and often affirming the negative Progressive narrative about America, they inadvertently convey the message that any public service, whether in government or the military, is not a noble and high calling to preserve liberty and justice for all but merely a defense of a nation illegitimately founded on institutional racism. Why would any sincere Christian want to become a public servant for such a nation?

Christians do not have the option to ignore politics. They should always support the candidate and party platform most closely aligned with biblical principles for providing fair, equal, and impartial justice. In reality, we only need a small percentage of Christians to step forward to serve in civil government, but the rest of the Christian church must support these individuals with their votes and resources. If the bench of candidates is weak, then Christians should work to identify, train, and support better candidates for the future.

Today, the Democratic Party has been completely taken over by the Progressive worldview, which fundamentally rejects the biblical principles behind the American founding. The Republican Party is by no means perfect, but its platform is clearly the most aligned with biblical principles for governing justly. Conversely, the current Democratic Party platform is contrary to the Moral Law on almost every count. The last several decades have shown they are united in pushing their party platform at every opportunity. Christians today must wrestle with this fact: when they vote for any Democrat, they are affirming a party platform that is diametrically opposed to their faith. This is the attitude they should have: "I cannot vote for a person or party whose platform stands in opposition to God's word." Sadly, they are not being taught this by their pastors and are largely ignorant of these points.

THE FOUNDERS DID NOT ABOLISH SLAVERY AND THOUGHT SLAVES WERE THREE-FIFTHS OF A PERSON

The charge from Progressives is that the founders believed slaves were worth only three-fifths of a person. This language is in the US Constitution in the section on representation in the new Congress. Additionally, some Progressives assert that the founders were primarily motivated to separate from England because they wanted to protect the institution of slavery. These beliefs have led to a general narrative that America's founding was systemically racist, and we are still suffering from this fundamental problem today. To address this, I will answer two questions:

1. What was the intent behind the three-fifths clause in the US Constitution?
2. What was the founders' intent regarding the institution of slavery?

Let us start with the three-fifths clause, which is found in the Constitution, Article 1, Section 2:

> Representatives and direct Taxes shall be apportioned among the several States which may be included within this Union, according to their respective Numbers, which shall be determined by adding to the whole Number of free Persons, including those bound to Service for a Term of Years, and excluding Indians not taxed, three fifths of all other Persons. . . . The Number of Representatives shall not exceed one for every thirty Thousand.[32]

The question being discussed was representation, and it was agreed that a representative would be assigned to every thirty thousand persons. Abolitionists saw a problem, however, with counting slaves at the same ratio as free persons. This same ratio would give pro-slavery states greater representation in the new federal government, making the abolition of slavery much more difficult.

There was also the moral problem of telling slaves they would have representation when those representing them would undoubtedly push to maintain their enslavement. Slaves were obviously whole people, and abolitionists sought to do whatever they could to end the horrific practice of slavery. The problem at the time, though, was that if slaves were counted with the same ratio as free people, their numbers would become a legislative advantage for the pro-slavery South.

James Wilson and Roger Sherman, both abolitionists, were the ones who proposed that instead of one representative for every thirty thousand slaves, the ratio should be one representative for every fifty thousand slaves, which is where "three-fifths" comes from. This ratio had been previously discussed in 1783 for property taxes, making the proposal easier to pass. With this adjusted ratio, slave-holding states would be incentivized to abolish slavery because doing so would immediately increase their representation in the new federal Congress.

Some people I talk with say they have heard this argument but are still not swayed by the idea that the three-fifths clause was intended to restrict the political power of the pro-slavery South. So, if the three-fifths strategy was indeed meant to hamper the efforts of the pro-slavery South, how did it play out?

Table A-1 displays the breakdown of representatives the North and South had with the three-fifths ratio applied. This approach granted the North about 55% representation, offering a significant political advantage. What people may not realize when suggesting that "slaves should have been counted at the same ratio as free persons" is that this would have given the South approximately nine more representatives in Congress, evenly splitting political power between free and slave-holding states. Would this have been beneficial for the abolitionist movement? Absolutely not.

Table A-1

Scenario	3/5ths	5/5ths	0/5ths
North # Representatives	58	58	58
South # Representatives	47	56	33
Total # Representatives	105	114	91
Northern % Reps in Congress	55%	51%	64%
Southern % Reps in Congress	45%	49%	36%

One could argue for an uncompromising stance, suggesting that slave-holding states should have received no representatives for their slaves (zero-fifths!), significantly curbing their political power and reducing the South's ratio in Congress to 36 percent. However, this proposal would have been rejected by Southern states, potentially jeopardizing the Constitution in its infancy and leaving the country to collapse under the Articles of Confederation. The three-fifths ratio emerged as an acceptable political compromise that provided Northern pro-abolition states with a substantial advantage in Congress while limiting the power of the pro-slavery South.

Some individuals with whom I share this struggle to acknowledge the true motive behind the three-fifths clause because it diverges from the Progressive narrative we have heard for decades. However, in examining the effect of the three-fifths clause, one can see that the numerical evidence demonstrating the northern political advantage supports the case. This clause resulted in reduced political power for the pro-slavery South.

As additional evidence supporting this interpretation of the fraction in the Constitution, consider the testimony of Frederick Douglass. Born a slave around 1820, he endured harsh treatment in his early years. Fleeing to the North to secure his freedom as a young man, he went on to become a successful businessman and a prominent spokesman for the abolitionist movement. In a speech he delivered in Glasgow, Scotland, on March 26, 1860, Douglass explained his perspective on the three-fifths clause:

> It is a downright disability laid upon the slaveholding States; one which deprives those States of two-fifths of their natural basis of representation. A black man in a free State is worth just two-fifths more than a black man in a slave State, as a basis of political power under the Constitution. Therefore, instead of encouraging slavery, the Constitution encourages freedom by giving an increase of "two-fifths" of political power to free over slave States. So much for the three-fifths clause; taking it at its worst, it still leans to freedom, not slavery; for, be it remembered that the Constitution nowhere forbids a coloured man to vote.[33]

Progressives reject Frederick Douglass' perspectives on this. Instead, they propagate the narrative that the founders believed slaves were three-fifths of a person to convince people that the founders were all racists with the intention of perpetuating the institution of slavery.

The next question to consider is: "Was the founders' objective in separating from England to institutionalize slavery?" It is true that leading up to the separation, one motivation of the Southern states was to protect their ability to maintain the institution of slavery. However, this was not the case for the majority of the founders. To demonstrate this, we will explore what the founders did, if anything, to end slavery during the founding era.

The key assumptions of the Progressive argument are that (1) nothing was done to end slavery in the founding era, and (2) any meaningful action to end slavery must occur at the federal level. Progressives assert that the new national government should have ended the practice right from the start. However, this point of view fails to recognize one of the most important realities of the new national government that formed after the Declaration of Independence in 1776: it had very little power. This was by design. The states were highly suspicious that the new federal government would impose tyranny on them, so the founders strictly limited the federal government's power. If slavery were to be dealt with at all, it would have to be addressed at the state level. So, did the states do anything to address slavery?

It turns out the states did a lot to end the institution of slavery, and their actions started well before the Declaration was signed. In 1775, the Pennsylvania Society for Promoting the Abolition of Slavery was founded, dedicated to the abolition of slavery. This early push was largely due to Quaker influence, which began in 1688 with the German Petition Against Slavery. At the time, this petition had little effect, but it is early evidence that there were colonials who believed slavery needed to be abolished.

With the writing of the Declaration, we see the next attempt to call out slavery as an example of the immoral rule of the king. Jefferson's first draft included twenty-eight examples of illegitimate rule on the part of King George, with the slave trade listed as one of the examples. Jefferson included this, being a slave owner in Virginia (the state with the most slaves by far*), as an example of why the colonies needed to separate from England because slavery was a legal practice across the British empire at that time:

> [H]e has waged cruel war against human nature itself, violating [its] most sacred rights of life & liberty in the persons of a distant people who never offended him, captivating & carrying them into slavery in another hemisphere, or to incur miserable death in their transportation thither. This piratical warfare, the opprobrium of infidel powers, is the warfare of the CHRISTIAN king of Great Britain. Determined to keep open a market where MEN should be bought & sold, he has prostituted his negative for suppressing every legislative attempt to prohibit or to restrain this execrable commerce: and that this assemblage of horrors might want no fact of distinguished die, he is now exciting those very people to rise in arms among us, and to purchase that liberty of which he has deprived them, & murdering the people upon whom he also obtruded them; thus paying off former crimes committed

---

* Virginia had ~39 percent of the slave population as of the 1790 census. https://en.wikipedia.org/wiki/1790_United_States_census

against the liberties of one people, with crimes which he urges them to commit against the lives of another.[34]

Unfortunately, the Southern states could not accept this language, leading to its removal in the final draft. Nevertheless, this writing reflects a growing concern about the lawfulness of the institution, even among slaveholders like Jefferson.

In 1787, several important measures were taken to stem the spread of slavery. One was the three-fifths clause in the US Constitution discussed earlier. Its intent was to limit the political power of the pro-slavery South and incentivize Southern states to abolish slavery because by doing so, they would immediately have greater representation in the new federal government. The second was the passing of the Northwest Ordinance, which applied to territories rather than new states. The new federal government had jurisdiction over US territories and included clear language about slavery in Article 6:

> There shall be neither slavery nor involuntary servitude in the said territory.[35]

This was passed before the Constitution was ratified, but upon ratification, the Northwest Ordinance was affirmed by the new Congress, along with a clear statement in Article 3 about teaching religion and morality:

> Religion, morality, and knowledge, being necessary to good government and the happiness of mankind, schools and the means of education shall forever be encouraged.[36]

More importantly, we must look at what the states did on their own, as they held the power to abolish slavery. The efforts of the Northern states show clearly their intent to end slavery, which they achieved through a series of laws over time, completely abolishing the practice by the mid-1800s.

Another attempt to abolish slavery occurred in 1790. In 1787, the Abolition Society, founded in 1775, appointed Ben Franklin as its president. Franklin, who had once owned slaves, had come to believe that slavery should be abolished. At the end of his life, on February 3, 1790, Franklin petitioned the new Congress to abolish slavery. This move came after the 1787 Constitutional Convention, where the delegates agreed not to attempt to pass federal legislation ending slavery for twenty years. Nevertheless, Franklin made a direct appeal to Congress with this declaration:

> That from a regard for the happiness of Mankind an Association was formed several years since in this State by a number of her Citizens of various religious denominations for promoting the Abolition of Slavery. . . . That mankind are all formed by the same Almighty being, alike objects of his Care & equally designed for the Enjoyment of *Happiness* the Christian Religion teaches us to believe & the Political Creed of America* fully coincides with the Position.[37]

---

* The reference to "Happiness" and "the Political Creed of America" is a direct reference to the Declaration of Independence and further recognizes the impact of principles captured in that document as foundational to the American Republic.

Lastly, in 1807, Congress passed the Act Prohibiting Importation of Slaves, which prohibited further importation of slaves. The US Coast Guard was tasked with patrolling to capture slave trading ships. This law took effect on January 1, 1808, immediately after the expiration of the twenty-year ban on any federal legislation regarding slavery, as specified in the Constitution. Clearly, the founders aimed to address this aspect of slavery as soon as the Constitution allowed, and they worked ahead of time to make it happen on the first day of the first year they could legally adopt it. Interestingly, the act was signed by then-president Thomas Jefferson, who had been unsuccessful in incorporating the slavery issue into the Declaration as one of the immoral policies protected by England.

The efforts and motives of the founding generation were summarized well by Abraham Lincoln in 1858 during his third debate with Stephen Douglas. Douglas's position was that America should stay "half slave and half free."[38] Lincoln argued the founders fully expected slavery to eventually be abolished:

> That is the exact difficulty between us. I say that Judge Douglas and his friends have changed them from the position in which our fathers originally placed it. I say, in the way our fathers originally left the slavery question, the institution was in the course of ultimate extinction, and the public mind rested in the belief that it was in the course of ultimate extinction.[39]

Clearly, there were many efforts across numerous states to end slavery. However, it took the Civil War many years later to finally overcome the support for slavery in the South. If we must identify the culprits for the sin of slavery in America, it is undoubtedly not the entire founding generation but rather a handful of leaders in the South who protected it despite the best efforts of many in the North to end it.

THE FOUNDERS WERE DEISTS

A deist is someone who acknowledges God but believes that God is not directly involved in the affairs of mankind. At the time of America's founding, deists typically showed little interest in God and Christianity, though they might have had respect for natural law as applied in civil matters. The claim that most of the founders were deists could significantly weaken the argument that America was founded on Christian principles and that these principles are crucial to maintain. This is because governing in a way that "honors God" would not matter to a deist, as they do not believe that God would intervene, even if they governed poorly. Therefore, the accusation that the founders were deists is a serious matter that requires investigation.

If the founders were deists, two primary behaviors would consistently be expected throughout the founding era and beyond. First, they would not pray or acknowledge God as directly affecting their lives. Second, they would not worry about God's judgment on the nation. However, numerous examples demonstrate that neither of these expectations was widely true during the founding era—in fact, we find the complete opposite.

Let us begin with the Declaration itself, specifically the concluding portion, which emphasizes the signers' reliance on God's protection to see the separation through:

> *Appealing to the Supreme Judge* of the World for the Rectitude of our Intentions. . . . With *a firm Reliance on the Protection of divine Providence,* we mutually pledge to each other our Lives, our Fortunes and our sacred Honor.[40]

For example, in a letter dated August 20, 1778, George Washington emphasized the role that God played when writing to Brigadier General Thomas Nelson:

> The *hand of Providence has been so conspicuous in all this,* that he must be worse than an infidel *that lacks faith,* and more than wicked, that has not gratitude enough to acknowledge his obligations.[41]

Another example of George Washington acknowledging the role that God played can be found in a letter dated November 15, 1781, written to the president of the Continental Congress, Thomas McKean:

> I take a particular Pleasure in acknowledging, that *the interposing Hand of Heaven in the various Instances* of our

extensive Preparations for this Operation, *has been most conspicuous & remarkable.*[42]

When George Washington officially resigned his military commission in Annapolis, Maryland, on December 23, 1783, he made the following statement about God's role in achieving independence:

> I resign with satisfaction the Appointment I accepted with diffidence—A diffidence in my abilities to accomplish so arduous a task, which however was superseded by a confidence in the rectitude of our Cause, the support of the Supreme Power of the Union, and the patronage of Heaven. . . . My *gratitude for the interposition of Providence,* and the assistance I have received from my Countrymen, increases with every review of the momentous Contest.[43]

During the Constitutional Convention in the summer of 1787, Benjamin Franklin made a direct reference to how God intervened in the struggle for independence:

> In the beginning of the Contest with G. Britain, when we were sensible of danger, *we had daily prayer in this room for Divine protection. Our prayers, Sir, were heard, & they were graciously answered.* All of us who were engaged in the struggle must have observed frequent instances of a super-intending Providence in our favor.[44]

In August of 1776, Samuel Adams wrote the following about how God was intervening in the colonials' struggle for independence:

> There are instances of, I would say, *an almost astonishing Providence in our favor; our success has staggered our enemies, and almost given faith to infidels;* so we may truly say *it is not our own arm which has saved us. The hand of Heaven appears to have led us on* to be, perhaps, humble instruments and means in the great providential dispensation, which is completing.[45]

In addition to this small sampling, there were dozens of prayer proclamations with the implied request that the citizens of the United States pray to God for provision and protection. Those attempting to argue that America was founded as a secular nation may find isolated statements to question the faith and motivation of the founders. However, the overall body of evidence unmistakably shows that the founders believed God was directing and blessing their cause, aligning them with Christianity and not with deism. While Europe was swept up in the Enlightenment and deistic thought, there is little evidence that the founders were deists.

One final note on deism: another definition of a deist is "one who professes no form of religion *but follows the light of nature and reason as his only guides in doctrine and practice.*"[46] In other words, mankind should be able to reason through and understand the laws of nature. This would allow them to explain these natural laws and apply them to improve daily living (i.e., using physics to advance architecture, or astronomy to improve navigation, or chemistry and biology to improve health). An atheist can do this while assuming there is no master designer, but so can a Christian. Only, when a Christian does it, they understand they are seeing God's handiwork in the universe He is purported to have created.

The Reformation period in the 1500s was the catalyst for methodical scientific study of the physical world as the Bible was translated into English so the masses could study it. The emergent idea was that there is a divine law created by God that is both moral and natural. The Moral Law is ultimately defined by the Bible; however, laws governing the universe can be discovered and known through reason. This theological breakthrough *is* what led to the greatest period of scientific discovery mentioned in Chapter 1.

This scientific approach to learning about God's creation has been pigeonholed to mean that a true scientist or engineer cannot also acknowledge an all-powerful creator who established the laws that mankind is encouraged to discover and use for the benefit of their fellow humans. The quotes from leading scientists provided in Chapter 1 demonstrate that there is no contradiction in a scientist or engineer seeking to understand the laws of nature and having faith in a God who is actively involved in the affairs of humanity.

As an engineer with forty years of experience in the industry, I see how the same principles echoed by famous scientists from centuries ago enable us to improve the human condition today. Studying the physical world around us continues to confirm a very precise design, implying the existence of a master designer. Given this, I view scientific discovery as akin to learning more about the creativity and genius of the God who created the universe.

Interestingly, both Jefferson and Franklin, two men most often labeled as deists, believed in a God who was involved in the affairs of men, yet they studied the natural laws like other famous scientists of that era. They were deists from a scientific standpoint, seeking to use reason to understand the laws of nature, but not from a theological standpoint, as one of my favorite Jefferson quotes proves:

> God who gave us life gave us liberty. And can the liberties of a nation be thought secure when we have removed their only firm basis, a conviction in the minds of the people that these liberties are of the Gift of God? That they are not to be violated but with His wrath? Indeed, I tremble for my country when I reflect that God is just; that His justice cannot sleep forever.[47]

SUMMARY

In my own journey of understanding the founding and studying all the common objections, it has become clear that while the founding generation was anything but perfect, they themselves also learning and working out their faith, most of them made heroic efforts to do the right thing *as they understood it at the time.* When examining a particular event and considering all sides, it becomes evident that the general movement during the founding era was to attempt to achieve the vision for civil government set forth in the Declaration of Independence: that all mankind has God-given rights, including the right to life, religious and civil liberty, and the pursuit of happiness, which they intended to mean pursuing God according to one's conscience.

In the end, it becomes clear that the motivation behind all these objections is to move us away from our founding covenant and the unique vision it describes. At the beginning of the twenty-first century, we find that those who reject our founding covenant have significantly weakened our nation's understanding and, as a result, the resolve to defend our national covenant. We find ourselves in the same situation as the founding generation and must decide on our course of action.

Who will step forward to lead us to a more just and fair society, one that truly aligns with biblical principles to provide liberty and justice for all? This is the same question asked in Ps. 94:16:

> Who will rise up for me against the wicked? Who will take
> a stand for me against evildoers?

Throughout history, people of faith have always believed that the Bible holds all the answers needed to live a purposeful life that honors God, including how to govern justly. We are the ones God calls to step forward and lead.

The duty is ours; the results are God's.[48]

APPENDIX II

THEOLOGY OF CIVIL GOVERNMENT

Many Pastors and church leaders are convinced that, regarding the role of Christians in politics today, the Bible teaches that Christians should focus on the Great Commission versus politics. Their theology can be summarized by two words: submit (Rom. 13) and pray (1 Tim. 2), regardless of how immoral or unjust the governing authorities are (see Table 2.1 in Chapter 2). The aim of this book has been to refute this theological position by providing clear biblical answers to the questions addressed in Chapters 1 through 5.

The intent of this section is to summarize a complete theological position regarding the role of Christians today in the communities and nations where they reside. Similar to a church's doctrinal statement of faith or any theological topic in a systematic theology textbook, this is accomplished through a series of statements of biblical truth with supporting verses spanning the Old and New Testaments:

1. God desires that people live in separate and sovereign nations spanning the globe (Gen. 9:1–7, 10:32, 11:1–9; Acts 17:26–28).
2. These nations are to be fruitful, increase in number, scatter across fill the earth, and govern justly, ultimately to learn about and pursue God (Gen. 1:28, 9:1–7, 10:1–32; Ps. 2:10–11, 66:7–9, 86:9, 108:3, 138:4–5; Acts 17:27; Matt. 28:18-20):
   - God expects his followers to step up to lead in their communities and nations to achieve these objectives and to receive His blessing (Exod. 18:20–22, 18:18–20; Jer. 22:15–16; Heb. 11:32–35).
   - This looks like supporting those attempting to govern justly, serving in their community if called, voting in all elections in alignment with biblical values, and including prayers for their community and national leaders (Exod. 18:20–22, 18:18–20; Isa. 10:1–2; Rom. 13:1–4; 1 Tim. 2:1–4).
3. The process to form a God-honoring community or nation is to establish a covenant through the free consent of the people (Exod. 19:7–8, 24:3), where they do the following:
   - Acknowledge there is a supreme ruler and judge of the universe (Exod. 20:18–20).
   - Appeal to this supreme ruler and judge for guidance and help (Exod. 3:7).
   - Commit through whatever legal process is appropriate for that culture (Exod. 19:7–8).
   - Declare it to the world (Exod. 24:5–7).

4. The operating principles God gives us to govern justly are as follows:

- Governments are established and maintained through a mutual covenant by the free consent of the people (Exod. 19:5–8; Acts 15:2; Titus 1:5).
- Governments are to embrace God's Moral Law as the standard to guide personal behavior and lawmaking (Exod. 20:1–17; Ps. 119; John 14:21; Rom. 13:1–4).
- Representative government consists of elected officials who promise to govern in accordance with God's Moral Law (Exod. 18:20–22, 18:18–20; Deut. 16:18–20, 17:18–20; Isa. 10:1–2).
- Legitimate rights of individuals must conform to the Moral Law. Chief among them are the following:
  - Life (Gen. 9:5–6; Exod. 20:13, 21:23; Lev. 24:17).
  - Liberty (Gen. 2:15–17; Ps. 81:11–14; Isa. 1:18; 1 Tim. 2:3–4; 2 Pet. 3:9; Rev. 20:7–8).
  - Pursuit of happiness, which means pursuing God as one's conscience dictates (Deut. 7:12–16, 12:7, 28:1–6, 33:28–29; Eccles. 2:26, 3:12; Ps. 119, 144:15; Matt. 5:3–12).
- Laws passed must be enforced through equal and impartial justice, where punishment matches the level of the crime (Exod. 21:22–25; Deut. 19:15–21; Lev. 24:17–22).
- Liberty is to be extended to all, regardless of religious belief (above).
- The community needs to be educated on these principles to enable everyone to live at peace with their

neighbor, which allows citizens to love their neighbor even if they have a different faith (Deut. 4:9–10; Eph. 6:4).

5. When a nation earnestly seeks to govern this way, God will bless them. But if they turn away from God and govern unjustly, God will judge that nation (Deut. 7:11–15, 11:26–28, 26:16-19, 28:1–14; Jer. 6:16–19; Ezek. 22:23–31; Ps. 33:8–22, 66:7–9, 81:11–14, 138:4–5; Mal. 3:1–5):
   - God tells Israel this repeatedly (Exod. 19:5–8; Deut. 8:19–20; Jer. 6:16–19; Jer. 22:15–16; Mal. 3:1–5).
   - God also tells this to Gentile nations (Jer. 6:16–19; Dan. 5:18–30; Jonah 1:2, 3:1–10).

6. Governing justly is God's timeless strategy to draw wayward nations to Him, ideally so they would follow Him (Deut. 4:5–8; 1 Kings 10:1–9, 23–25; 2 Chron. 9:1–8, 22-24; Acts 17:26–27):
   - God's original purpose for Israel was to be a light to the Gentile nations, meaning they could learn about God through Israel. To facilitate this, He placed Israel on the only natural land bridge connecting the nearby continents making them the crossroads of civilization (Deut. 4:5–8, 1 Kings 10:4–5, Matt. 12:39–42).
   - The reason people around the world have been drawn to America is because they are drawn by and seek freedom that our system of government uniquely provides.

7. When the civil authority is governing justly, Christians should submit and pray for their civil leaders (Rom. 13:1–5; 1 Pet. 2:13–17; 1 Tim. 2:1–4). This means the government is doing the following:

- Passing laws in harmony with the Moral Law (Exod. 18:20–22, 18:18–20; Isa. 10:1–2).
- Providing equal, fair, and impartial justice for all (Deut. 16:18–20, 24:17–18, 27:19; Ps. 82:3–4; 1 Kings 10:9; Lev. 19:15; Prov. 17:15).
- Respecting the institutions God has ordained for all nations:
  - Marriage and family: recognizing God created us male and female, and respecting the role of father, mother, and children (Gen. 1:27, 2:18–25, 5:2; Exod. 20:12; Eph. 5:25–33, 6:4).
  - Civil government: respecting the founding covenant and operating principles (Gen. 9:5–6; Rom. 13:1–4; 1 Pet. 2:13–17).
  - Church: acknowledging its role as a steward of God's word, guiding the destiny of individuals, communities, and nations (Acts 17:26–28; Matt. 16:18–19, 28:18–20).

8. When the civil authority denies justice and abuses their citizens, denying them of their God-given rights and/ or abusing the key institutions God has instituted, then God's followers have a duty to act as follows:

- Using the legal system to secure justice: two prostitutes claiming the same baby as their own (1 Kings

3:16–28), the widow seeking justice (Luke 18:1–8), and Paul seeking justice (Acts 25:8–12).

- Calling out civil leaders directly: Old Testament prophets like Nathan (2 Sam. 12:7–9), John the Baptist (Matt. 14:1–12, Luke 3:19–20), and Jesus (Matt. 23:23).

- Civil disobedience as seems prudent: Daniel (Dan. 6:10–13); Shadrach, Meshach, and Abednego (Dan. 3:8–30); the Apostles (Acts 5:27–29).

- Silence equals consent: God will judge those remaining silent (Esther 4:12–14; Lev. 19:17, 20:4–5; Ezek. 9:1–10; Num. 20:8–12, 30:1-8; Prov. 24:10–12, 29:24).

9. When a governing authority denies justice and abuses their citizens with unjust laws over a long period of time with no intent to govern justly, they forfeit their God-given authority to rule. In this case, it is the right and duty of God's followers to "throw off such Government, and to provide new Guards for their future Security,"[49] as seems prudent based on their circumstances:

- Individual self-defense, defending you *or* your neighbor from an assailant (Exod. 22:2; Neh. 4:14; Ps. 144:1; Matt. 24:43; Luke 22:36; Rom. 12:18).

- Protecting one's family from an intruder, like a foreign nation or a tyrannical government (Exod. 22:2–3, Luke 11:21, 22:36, 1 Tim 5:8).

- God judges sinful nations: for example, Sodom, Edom, Canaanites, Babylonians, and Israel when they strayed

(Gen. 19:1–29, Oba 1:1–21, Lev. 18:24–27, Gen. 15:13–21, Isa. 13:1–14:23, Jer. 6:18–19, 11:6–8).

10. If a wayward nation realizes its offense toward God and wishes to seek restoration, it must follow the same four-step process: *acknowledging* its sin, *appealing* to God for help, *recommitting* to their covenant, and *declaring* it to the world:

- Israel recommitment examples: Moses (Deut. 29:2–15), Solomon (1 Kings 8:22–66; 2 Chron. 7:14), Josiah (2 Kings 23:1–3), Nehemiah (Neh. 9:3, 38).
- Gentile example nations: Nineveh (Jonah 1:2, 3:1–10), Babylon under Nebuchadnezzar (Dan. 4:1–37).

ENDNOTES

[1] William Federer, *America's God and Country Encyclopedia of Quotations* (St. Louis: Amerisearch, Inc., 2000), p. 15, quoted in David Barton, The Wallbuilder Report (Aledo, TX: Wallbuilder Press, Summer 1993), p. 3.

[2] William Federer, *America's God and Country Encyclopedia of Quotations.*

[3] Nicolaus Copernicus, William Federer, "Faith of Famous, and a church organist discovering a planet," *American Minute* (blog), August 21, 2023, https://americanminute.com/blogs/todays-american-minute/faith-of-famous-astronomers-and-a-church-organist-discovering-a-planet-sir-william-herschel-american-minute-with-bill-federer.

[4] Galileo Galilei, William Federer, "Faith of Famous, and a church organist discovering a planet."

[5] Johannes Kepler, "Johannes Kepler Quote," https://libquotes.com/johannes-kepler/quote/lbf4z9c, quoted in Morris Kline, *Mathematical Thought from Ancient to Modern Times*, p. 231.

[6] Francis Bacon, *Novum Organum*, originally published 1620, (1c Kings Road, Whithorn, Newton Stewart, Dumfries & Galloway, Anodos Books, 2019), p. 120.

[7] William Federer, *America's God and Country Encyclopedia of Quotations* (St. Louis: Amerisearch, Inc., 2000), p. 493, quoted in John Hudson Tiner, *Louis Pasteur: Founder of Modern Medicine* (Milford, Michigan: Mott Media, Inc., 1990), p. 75.

[8] *An American Dictionary of the English Language* (1828), s.v. "right."

[9] James Otis, "The Rights of the British Colonies Asserted and Proved," Online Library of Liberty, 1763, https://oll.libertyfund.org/page/1763-otis-rights-of-british-colonies-asserted-pamphlet.

[10] "Divine right of kings," Wikipedia, last modified August 22, 2021, https://en.wikipedia.org/wiki/Divine_right_of_kings.

[11] Charles Ryrie, *Basic Theology: A Popular Systematic Guide to Understanding Biblical Truth* (Chicago: Moody Publishers, 1986), p. 441, 444.

[12] Charles Ryrie, *Basic Theology: A Popular Systematic Guide to Understanding Biblical Truth*, p. 444.

[13] Thomas Jefferson, "An Act for Establishing Religious Freedom," Encyclopedia Virginia, January 16, 1786, https://encyclopediavirginia.org/entries/an-act-for-establishing-religious-freedom-1786/.

[14] "The Mayflower Compact," https://themayflowersociety.org/history/the-mayflower-compact/.

[15] "The Mayflower Compact."

[16] "The Mayflower Compact."

[17] "The Mayflower Compact."

[18] Thomas Jefferson, "The Declaration of Independence," 1776, https://www.archives.gov/founding-docs/declaration-transcript

[19] William Blackstone, *Blackstone's Commentaries on the Laws of England*, The Avalon Project, 1765https://avalon.law.yale.edu/18th_century/blackstone_intro.asp#2.

[20] James Otis, "The Rights of the British Colonies Asserted and Proved."

[21] John Jay, "Sermons and Biblical Studies," https://www.biblia.work/sermons/jayjohn/.

[22] Thomas Jefferson, "The Declaration of Independence."

[23] Thomas Jefferson, "The Declaration of Independence."

[24] Dr. Larry P. Arnn, *The Founders' Key: The Divine and Natural Connection Between the Declaration and the Constitution and What We Risk by Losing It* (Nashville: Thomas Nelson, 2012), p. 5.

25 William Federer, *America's God and Country Encyclopedia of Quotations.*

26 William Ely Hill, "My Wife and My Mother-in-Law," *Puck Magazine,* November 6, 1915, https://www.loc.gov/resource/cph.3b45252/.

27 William Federer, *America's God and Country Encyclopedia of Quotations.*

28 Everson v. Board of Education, 330 U.S. 1 (1947).

29 Thomas Jefferson, "Jefferson's Letter to the Danbury Baptists," Library of Congress, January 1, 1802, https://www.loc.gov/loc/lcib/9806/danpre.html.

30 Thomas Jefferson, "From Thomas Jefferson to Samuel Miller, 23 January 1808," National Archives, January 23, 1808, https://founders.archives.gov/documents/Jefferson/99-01-02-7257.

31 Runkel v. Winemiller, 4 H. & McH. 429 (1799).

32 U.S. Constitution, art. I, section II.

33 "(1860) Frederick Douglass, 'The Constitution of the United States: Is It Pro-Slavery or Anti-Slavery?,'" BlackPast, March 15, 2012, https://www.blackpast.org/global-african-history/1860-frederick-douglass-constitution-united-states-it-pro-slavery-or-anti-slavery/.

34 Thomas Jefferson, "The Declaration of Independence." Thomas Jefferson's original Draft of the Declaration of Independence, https://www.loc.gov/exhibits/declara/ruffdrft.html.

35 "Northwest Ordinance," National Archives, 1787, https://www.archives.gov/milestone-documents/northwest-ordinance.

36 "Northwest Ordinance."

37 "Petition from the Pennsylvania Society for the Abolition of Slavery," ushistory.org, February 3, 1790, https://www.ushistory.org/documents/antislavery.htm.

38 "Lincoln–Douglas Third Debate," Abraham Lincoln Historical Society, http://www.abraham-lincoln-history.org/lincoln-douglas-3nd-debate-jonesboro-illinois-reply/.

39 "Lincoln-Douglas Third Debate."

[40] Thomas Jefferson, "The Declaration of Independence."

[41] George Washington, "From George Washington to Brigadier General Thomas Nelson, Jr., 20 August 1778," National Archives, August 20, 1778, https://founders.archives.gov/documents/Washington/03-16-02-0373.

[42] George Washington, "From George Washington to Thomas McKean, 15 November 1781," National Archives, November 15, 1781, https://founders.archives.gov/documents/Washington/99-01-02-07409.

[43] "From George Washington to United States Congress, 23 December 1783," National Archives, December 23, 1783, https://founders.archives.gov/documents/Washington/99-01-02-12223.

[44] David Barton and Tim Barton, *The American Story: The Beginnings* (Wallbuilder Press, 2021), p. 211.

[45] Samuel Adams, "Speech about the Declaration of Independence – 1776," Samuel Adams Heritage Society, August 1, 1776, http://www.samuel-adams-heritage.com/documents/speech-about-declaration-of-independence.html.

[46] *An American Dictionary of the English Language* (1828), s.v. "Deist."

[47] Thomas Jefferson, Notes on the State of Virginia, Query XVIII, 237, quoted in William J. Federer, *America's God and Country Encyclopedia of Quotations* (St. Louis: Amerisearch, Inc., 2000).

[48] William Federer, *America's God and Country Encyclopedia of Quotations*.

[49] Thomas Jefferson, "The Declaration of Independence."

ABOUT THE AUTHOR

Mark is originally from Pennsylvania and grew up in the Episcopal Church where he accepted Christ as a teenager. He attended Penn State University and met his wife, Charlene, in 1980. They married in 1983 and, a year later, moved to northeast Pennsylvania where Mark began his career in the private sector. While living there, they helped start several independent Bible churches that continue today.

In 1987, Mark developed a mentoring relationship with an experienced pastor and spent several years studying systematic theology. In the early 1990s, he began a teaching ministry covering a variety of topics, and in the late '90s, he became interested in biblical aspects of the American founding.

His first book, *Rediscovering the American Covenant: Roadmap to Restore America*, covers the history and theology that informed the founding and addresses many of the objections to active citizenship pastors and church leaders have. This book takes a simplified approach by answering five basic questions many are asking regarding what the Bible truly teaches about citizenship.

Referencing thousands of verses, Mark argues that Christians have a citizenship duty in the communities and nations where they live. Their primary objective is to establish liberty and justice for all so a community may live in peace. This enables everyone to go on their own personal faith journey at their own pace without coercion by any individual or institution. This is the responsibility of every Christian: *The Duty Is Ours*.